UNDERSTANDING POVERTY IN THE CLASSROOM

Changing Perceptions for Student Success

Beth Lindsay Templeton

ROWMAN & LITTLEFIELD EDUCATION

A division of
ROWMAN & LITTLEFIELD PUBLISHERS, INC.
Lanham • New York • Toronto • Plymouth, UK

Published by Rowman & Littlefield Education
A division of Rowman & Littlefield Publishers, Inc.
A wholly owned subsidary of
The Rowman & Littlefield Publishing Group, Inc.
4501 Forbes Boulevard, Suite 200, Lanham, Maryland 20706
http://www.rowmaneducation.com

Estover Road, Plymouth PL6 7PY, United Kingdom

British Library Cataloguing in Publication Information Available

Library of Congress Cataloging-in-Publication Data

Templeton, Beth Lindsay, 1948-
    Understanding poverty in the classroom : changing perceptions for student
    success / Beth Lindsay Templeton.
        p. cm.
    Includes bibliographical references.
    ISBN 978-1-61048-363-6 (cloth : alk. paper) — ISBN 978-1-61048-364-3
(pbk. : alk. paper) — ISBN 978-1-61048-365-0 (ebook)
    1. Academic achievement—United States. 2. School improvement
programs—United States. 3. Poor children—Education—United States.
4. Minorities—Education—United States. I. Title.
LB1062.6.T46 2011
371.826'9420973—dc22

                                                                      2011001372

∞™ The paper used in this publication meets the minimum requirements of
American National Standard for Information Sciences—Permanence of Paper
for Printed Library Materials, ANSI/NISO Z39.48-1992.

Printed in the United States of America

For Lindsay, Michael, Ella, and Sam
May you be blessed with teachers who nurture the spark of learning
for your entire lives.

CONTENTS

PART III   SUCCESS IS POSSIBLE

ACKNOWLEDGMENTS

I would like to offer thanks to Rhonda Corley, who asked for us in 1993 to develop "training related to children of homeless families," and to Ashley King who, as a summer intern in 2004, took that material and developed the draft prototype for the workshop "Understanding Poverty in the Classroom."

Thank you, Olivia Morris, for your support and advocacy with the school district.

A big thank-you to all the teachers, administrators, counselors, and school specialists who allowed me the privilege of deepening your awareness of poverty in your schools. You have shared with me and expanded my own knowledge immensely.

A special appreciation is for the woman known as Abby in the conclusion of this book. Your bravery and accomplishments make me proud to be acquainted with you. Thank you for sharing your story.

Thanks to R.J. March for working with me as we tried to sensitize others to poverty issues so they can reach out with wisdom and compassion. Your passion for people of low wealth, coupled with your considerable skills and talents, are powerful. Thanks for having been my colleague.

Tammi Hart, you came into my life at just the right time. Thank you for easing my frustration handling manuscript details. You are a true partner in this journey of helping others understand poverty.

I am also grateful to Scott Henderson and Lesley Quast of the Education Department of Furman University for their affirmation that "Understanding Poverty in the Classroom" as a workshop and then as a book was vital to their developing teachers.

And to my husband, parents, children, and grandchildren, thanks for supporting me in the work that I am called to do. You make it easier for me to follow my passion.

Beth Lindsay Templeton
October 2010

INTRODUCTION

Why this book at this time? In our public schools, we are seeing a greater number of students who live in poverty. The majority of students in many schools are on free and reduced lunch programs. In fact, in nine states (including the District of Columbia), more than 50% of children in public schools qualify for free and reduced lunches (Florida Department of Education, 2009). Another twelve states have rates of 40% or more. More often than not, teachers are middle class with the worldview of middle-class people. The classroom can be a difficult place for low-income students who may understand the world differently.

Teachers want to be the person mentioned when a former student stands up and says, "My life was changed forever by being a student in [teacher's name]'s classroom!" Children who come from poverty need and deserve the best that our education systems can offer. To connect with children who live in poverty, educators need to understand the experiences, backgrounds, and realities of these students. Teachers want to teach, and students want to learn.

At the end of my workshop "Understanding Poverty in the Classroom," one teacher said, "I wish more teachers had this training. We would have fewer teachers burn out." This book addresses the harmful and sometimes frustrating misunderstandings that result from socioeconomic differences in and beyond the classroom.

Understanding Poverty in the Classroom: Changing Perceptions for Student Success will help teachers identify perceptual differences between children with resources and those who are accustomed to living with limited resources. Teachers will gain an awareness of how these perceptions can be more sensitive because of cultural and socioeconomic differences. This resource provides teaching strategies that address the special needs of children who live in poverty and encourages teachers to learn about the neighborhoods in which their students live and what to look for in those areas. The book also helps teachers confront myths about poverty and homelessness and learn how to find factual demographic information about poverty.

Teachers go into teaching so that they can change the world. However, many of them are not adequately prepared in their initial teacher training or provided ongoing professional development for the actual students they encounter. They don't understand the importance of a student being able to physically defend himself or herself or why a child may have $100 athletic shoes but is on a free and reduced lunch program. They do not realize that children are unable to pay attention to the structure of the classroom lesson until they are certain that the teacher likes them.

Without understanding the realities of their students' lives, even with great intentions, teachers can make bad situations worse. For example, a student may be very loud and have the tendency to interrupt class. The teacher can strongly discipline the student for behavior that appears to be rude or defiant of authority. However, when teachers understand that a child who lives in an overcrowded situation learns to interrupt often and loudly to survive, they come to realize that the child is not being disrespectful but just living out lessons learned at home. Rather than punishing, a teacher can use the opportunity to demonstrate other options for appropriate behavior without being critical of family codes.

Likewise, without understanding the situation, a teacher may grow to dislike students because their perceived lack of responsibility is just irresponsible. Teachers may lament, "They never have their homework," "They never return papers signed," "Their parents never show up for meetings," or "They smell bad all the time." These and other frustrations lead teachers to disconnect from their students and be ineffective because of their own inability to see the behavior in its fuller context of poverty-related realities. Teachers are not choosing to be judgmental when it comes to fully engaging their students. They simply have never learned any other way to look at their pupils and the conditions in which they live.

Finally, most teachers have a real passion for educating their students. They go beyond the expectations of their administrators. They use their own money for supplies and special treats. They love their chosen vocation. But they don't know what to do to help their students because they've never experienced what their pupils have. Many teachers have not had to wonder if the house they slept in last night will be the one they sleep in tonight. They have not had to cook for their five-year-old sister and two-year-old brother when they were only eight years old themselves. They have not had to worry that their mother is never home because she works three part-time jobs just to keep a roof over their heads. They have not been told to get off the school bus, go in the house, lock the door, and not come out until Mama gets home at 10:00 p.m. And because they cannot relate to these challenges, teachers simply don't know what to do. Their hearts are engaged, but their minds need more insight to be truly effective teachers.

This book grew out of workshops presented to teachers of all grades, kindergarten through high school. After you read this book, you may choose to organize a group of teachers to discuss the lessons provided here. Adults learn best in small groups with the opportunity for extensive interaction. After absorbing this information and incorporating it into your teaching life, you will be the teacher who hears years later that you were the changing point for students in your classroom. Without you, their lives would not have been the same.

I

UNDERSTANDING POVERTY

(1)

DEFINING THE WELL-BEING
OF A CHILD

Good educational principles state that to achieve success, we must define our goal. To help both children who live in poverty and the teacher responsible for them to succeed in the classroom, we need to define what we hope to accomplish. The real goal for teachers is to nurture the well-being of a child so that he or she can attain maximum potential. We want students to thrive both as children and later on as adults.

MEASURING WELL-BEING

Beyond learning the basics of reading, writing, and mathematics, what is it that the educational system really wants for its students? Mastery of facts? Test scores? The ability to learn? Are schools interested in the overall well-being of children? How will we know when children are truly thriving? What do we mean by well-being? Without defining what well-being is, we have no way of knowing if we have accomplished it in the lives of children.

According to the Funders' Network for Smart Growth and Livable Communities, the well-being of a child means that that child is free of disease and injury, is in good physical health, has good social and emotional functioning, and has good cognitive development (adapted from Vandivere, Hair, Theokas, Cleveland, NcNamara, and Atienza, 2006).

The Every Child Matters Education Fund (2008) measures child well-being in the 50 states based upon the following measures:

- infant mortality
- child deaths, ages 1 to 14
- teen deaths, ages 15 to 20
- births to teen mothers
- late or no prenatal care
- child poverty
- uninsured children
- juvenile incarceration
- child abuse deaths
- child welfare expenditures
- total tax burden (reflects the overall federal, state, and local tax burden)

When we look at state rankings for child well-being, we see that geography matters for children. The five states that best provide for children's well-being at the time of this writing are Vermont, Massachusetts, Connecticut, Rhode Island, and New Hampshire. The worst five are South Carolina, Texas, Oklahoma, New Mexico, and Mississippi (Every Child Matters Education Fund, 2008).

A dismal ranking based on the previous list does not have to be a *prescription* for children in these states. The ranking is merely a *description* of which areas require improvement. We can address the well-being of children when we have a clear understanding of the definition of well-being.

When looking at the measures that various studies have used to quantify well-being, we discover that the categories tend to coalesce around four areas: (1) having a healthy start in life, (2) being healthy, (3) having well-developed social and emotional functioning, and (4) having the ability to learn. Let's explore each of these categories a bit further.

Having a Healthy Start in Life

A fundamental underpinning for the well-being of children is that they have a good start in life. This means, in part, that their mothers are healthy. They receive adequate prenatal care and live in homes free from toxins, pests, and unsafe conditions. Moms are also properly educated, since one predictor of a child's success in school is the education level of his or her mother (Liz Library, 2009).

Getting a good start has close correlation with the level of schooling achieved by a child's parents. The National Center for Children in Poverty (2010) reports that "among children whose parents work full-time and year-round, 74% of children whose parents have less than a high school diploma live in low-income families; 45% of children whose parents have a high school diploma but no college education live in low-income families; [and] only 16% of children whose parents have some college education or more live in low-income families" (n.p.).

In fact, the higher the parents' educational level, the higher the chance of a child's sense of well-being. Child Trends (2010) reports that "higher levels of parent educational attainment are strongly associated with positive outcomes for children in many areas, including school readiness; educational achievement; incidence of low birth weight; health-related behaviors, including smoking and binge drinking; and prosocial activities, such as volunteering. Children of more educated parents arc also likely to have access to greater material, human, and social resources" (n.p.).

Being Healthy

We also know that child well-being depends on being healthy. Some birth defects have a genetic link, while others are tied to the mother's health practices—whether she does drugs, drinks, or smokes, and whether she has a healthy diet. Children born with birth defects begin life with significant challenges to leading stable, secure, and wholesome lives

Good health means receiving regular checkups as an infant and toddler, along with getting the appropriate inoculations. Access to pre-scribed medications and appropriate therapies also greatly improves a child's health. It means having an adequate and nutritious diet. It means enjoying the opportunity to be physically active in normal child play to develop gross motor skills. Freedom from living in a physically abusive situation adds to children's good health.

A child's health is connected to living in an environment that minimizes accidents and injuries. Having a home that is free of mold, mildew, dander, bugs, rodents, and toxic chemicals reduces the risks of asthma and other respiratory illnesses. Children who are healthy exhibit a sense of well-being.

Having Well-Developed Social and Emotional Functioning

Children with a strong sense of well-being exhibit fully developed emotional and social functioning. When the behavior modeled for them by the adults in their lives is abusive, loud, aggressive, and demeaning, children may not get along well with others. They may not know how to interact in an appropriate manner with children of their same age.

If children live in an environment that is overcrowded, they may learn to talk loudly so they can be heard. They may have the tendency to interrupt, because that's how communication is carried out at home. They may have few personal boundaries. On the other hand, if they live in an overcrowded situation, they may be extremely meek and reticent to engage with anyone, because they learned that "disappearing" behavior at home is safest.

When children do not have the opportunity to make decisions on their own, they may have underdeveloped emotional and social functioning. They learn that they must do whatever they are told to do, no matter how inconsistent or irrational those instructions may be. They may not know how to initiate positive interactions with others, because they have never had the opportunity to do so or been shown how to do it.

Children may be stunted emotionally by regularly receiving such negative messages as, "You never do it right," "I don't know why you are so stupid," "You'll never amount to anything," "You're just like your father," "I didn't succeed, so I know you won't either," or "I can't believe that you did that." Without positive reinforcements or opportunities for success, children will believe the negative comments they hear and quit trying. They will bury the best parts of themselves to try to avoid confrontation, conflict, or anxiety. A happy and confident child is a child with a strong sense of well-being.

Having the Ability to Learn

A child who exhibits a sense of well-being can learn. She has been exposed to the joys of learning from an early age. As a toddler, she was not just given a ball, she was given a *big blue* ball and then a *little green* ball. Learning was part of play. Reading was a visible part of each day, because the parent read for herself and then read to her daughter or son, even if the topic was street signs or storefronts.

Children with a strong sense of well-being learn how to learn and make decisions. They know how to complete a task step by step because they followed a process when they helped bake cookies or learned rituals for getting up in the morning and leaving for school on time. Children who enjoy well-being have been given the opportunity to solve problems instead of always being told what to do, when to do it, and how to do it. Even children with overprotective parents do not learn how to solve problems, because Mom or Dad is always right there to take charge.

A mantra that is helpful with not only adults but also your own children is, "Do not ever do for someone what he/she can do for himself/herself." When we do something for others rather than letting them try, we inadvertently convey the message "I don't think you can do this." And they prove us right. They can't do this—now or in the future. We have not given them the opportunity to learn and succeed.

When we instill in children a sense of competence, we and other adults in their lives help them develop skills in mathematics, literacy, and technology. They learn the basics for successful living. With a sense of competence, children gain reading skills and gain decision-making power in their lives. They learn how not to be taken advantage of. They read to expand their worlds and comprehend the instructions they are given on the job as adults. They learn mathematics skills to think logically and rationally; progress in their careers; handle household expenses, loans, bills, and savings options; and know when someone is trying to cheat them.

Children who exhibit a sense of well-being learn technology skills so they can be part of life in the twenty-first century. They learn how to access information, produce documents, and stay in touch with the global community. They are productive and competent.

With a clear sense of children's well-being, we learn that helping students to succeed means more than opening their heads and pouring in information that they can give back to us. Education means nurturing those characteristics of well-being that we can effect in the classroom: supporting health, developing confidence, improving emotional and social functioning, and developing competence and productivity. By understanding how poverty can negatively impact the sense of a child's well-being, we can be more attentive to changing or improving our methods to enhance the lives of all students.

(2)

POVERTY IN OUR MIDST

When we work with students who live in poverty, we can often identify that the underpinnings for a sense of well-being may be lacking.
However, we must also acknowledge that we may not fully understand
or appreciate the strengths present in and positive experiences of these
students. We look at them through our own ways of understanding life
and relationships, and miss opportunities for powerful teaching and
interaction. We simply misunderstand or misinterpret what we are wit-
nessing.

UNDERSTANDING POVERTY

Depending on where you live, you may never see poverty in the normal
routine of your day. You may live in a financially stable neighborhood.
You may drive on streets that meander through vibrant business districts, easily obtain the fresh foods that your family enjoys, and attend
worship with people who share similar viewpoints. You may shop in
well-maintained stores and socialize with people whose education level
is akin to yours. Your car might be relatively new. All in all, you may be
able to readily avoid seeing or knowing about poverty in your school or
community.

Conversely, some of you may live in a place where you cannot avoid regular confrontations with the realities of poverty. You may even be used to seeing dilapidated housing, boarded up stores, and trash-strewn roadways. You may pass through these areas on your way home but don't really see the community anymore. You may ask why anyone bothers addressing the issue because no one cares or can solve the problem anyway. As a result, you put your blinders on and keep on going.

Some of you may see what is going on around you and allow your hearts to be broken on a regular basis. You may want to do something but feel powerless. You may want others to know what you know. You may accept that you need more information about what is going on in your community if you are going to help friends and colleagues change their minds and look at your area the way you do.

All of us who are fortunate enough to have the education and resources to use this book have holes in our learning about those who live in poverty. Whether we are ignorant of poverty in our community, blind to it, or overwhelmed by it, we nevertheless can learn about people whose experiences and knowledge bases are different from ours. We can place ourselves in situations that help us experience in our minds, hearts, and bodies—in a small way—some issues of poverty that children in our schools know too well.

To deepen your understanding of poverty in the classroom, this book includes exercises to help you expand your way of thinking. You can skip the exercises or come back to them later, but if you do them as they appear, you will experience their impact more powerfully.

GETTING TO KNOW YOU

This exercise is fun to do. If you're using this material in a group setting, enjoy getting to know each other. Invite two or three people to answer these questions for themselves and then share. Answer the following questions before moving ahead.

 1. Where did your family gather for discussions when you were a child?

2. What is/was the punishment of choice in your home?
3. Who was your favorite family member? Why?
4. What size shoes do you wear?
5. What did you eat for dinner last night?
6. What was your favorite game or toy?

Did you enjoy walking down memory lane? Did you notice that your age affected how you answered certain questions? If you are an older adult, the punishment of choice in your family might have been spanking. If you are a younger adult, you probably did not experience corporal punishment. You may have been given time-outs or grounding restrictions or denied privileges. Favorite toys or games may also be generational. Playing outside until dark has been replaced with playing video games. While none of this is good or bad, it is worth noting.

Now let's look at the questions through the eyes of someone whose upbringing is different. People who have lived in poverty for most of their lives may have a difficult time answering these questions. Rather than being an enjoyable exercise, this process may have been painful. Let's look at the questions again.

1. Where Did Your Family Gather for Discussions When You Were a Child?

Families who move a lot or experience significant disruption may not have a gathering place. They may not have family discussions, because no one realizes the importance of input from everyone. They may never be home at the same time. Or they are too stressed to talk calmly and gently with each other. They may not have a kitchen table to gather around. They may have moved around so much that when they close their eyes they see no place as being "home." When you have no "home," you cannot identify a gathering place for that home.

2. What Is/Was the Punishment of Choice in Your Home?

The punishment of choice might be brutal, including beatings, whippings, or being locked out of the house overnight. One young woman revealed that her punishment as a child was to be given to her brothers for them to do anything they chose with her—anything. She now struggles with addiction, relationship issues, and low self-esteem. Others have shared stories of being locked in a closet or deprived of food as their regular punishment.

3. Who Was Your Favorite Family Member? Why?

A favorite family member for some of the children in your classroom might be whoever is living in the house at the time. The family configuration changes so often and the family moves so many times that forming any kind of significant attachment is difficult. Children with these experiences may have difficulty creating and holding on to friendships at school.

4. What Size Shoes Do You Wear?

People who get their footwear out of boxes of donated shoes or at a thrift store might not know their shoe size. If a child has only had shoes that have been handed down to him, he will not know his shoe size. He is only interested in whether the shoe fits.

5. What Did You Eat for Dinner Last Night?

There may have been no supper last night. Or it may have been a candy bar. Or it may have been whatever was in the cabinet—no matter how inappropriate. Supper may have been whatever the oldest child in the family, even if that child is only six years old, could put on the table for the rest of the kids.

6. What Was Your Favorite Game or Toy?

Moving around a lot means that possessions get lost, thrown away, or destroyed. When a family is evicted, all their belongings can end up along the side of the road. If a family leaves their dwelling in the middle of the night to get away from an abusive situation or avoid a landlord, then family members take only what they can carry in their hands. Favorite toys have no significance to the adults in the household in this kind of stressful living situation; therefore, you may notice that a child at school attaches to a coat, book bag, or any other object that provides a bit of security.

The questions are the same, but the answers are vastly different. Our economic background affects how we perceive the world. We cannot assume that others see life in the ways that we do, because our experiences, families, education, and economics are different. We understand realities through different filters.

POVERTY DEMOGRAPHICS

Learning about poverty statistics, such as, the poverty rate in our area, federal poverty guidelines, the percentage of people without education or medical support, the percentage of children living in poverty, and so forth, can help us see beyond our everyday world. Harsh numbers can speak profoundly about a problem and reinforce its reality in our communities. Numbers can help us acknowledge that we have a problem when it is not highly visible. For example, your town may have little or no visible homelessness, but researchers and providers of homeless services might know at least 1,000 people who are homeless each night in your city. These numbers can teach you what your own experiences cannot.

Poring over a list of numbers can be boring and overwhelming. Because teachers love tests—to give them, not to take them—the following is a poverty test to help you learn more about poverty. The numbers are national. The answers cite sources where you can find information about your own county.

THE POVERTY TEST

Circle the correct answer for each question.

1. The 2010 federal poverty level for a family of four was _____.
   a. $17,600 or below
   b. $22,050 or below
   c. $24,800 or below

Answer: b.

Source: U.S. Department of Health and Human Services (2010). This figure is updated in February of each year; however, the Obama administration is reconsidering the formula for determining the poverty guidelines. See the answer for question 11 for the current formula.

2. In 2009, the percentage and number of U.S. residents living at or below the poverty level was _____.
   a. 9.5% (2.9 million)
   b. 14.3% (4.37 million)
   c. 18.4% (5.6 million)

Answer: b.

Source: National Poverty Center (2009).

3. Based on Housing and Urban Development (HUD) guidelines that no more than 30% of a household's income should go toward rent/mortgage, a worker earning minimum wage ($7.25 per hour) can afford a rent of _____.
   a. $377 per month
   b. $402 per month
   c. $539 per month

Answer: a.

Source: National Low Income Housing Coalition (2009). This report provides housing information for any county, metropolitan area, or state. It is a great resource for finding out specifics about your own area.

4. Using the HUD standard that no more than 30% of a household's income should go toward rent, what is the hourly wage needed to afford a two-bedroom apartment with the fair market rate rent of $757?
   a. $7.67 per hour
   b. $9.14 per hour
   c. $11.28 per hour

Answer: c.

Source: National Low Income Housing Coalition (2009).

5. The annual income required to afford a two-bedroom fair market rate apartment with a rent of $757 in 2009 was _____.
   a. $18,000
   b. $25,960
   c. $30,280

Answer: b.

Source: National Low Income Housing Coalition (2009).

6. Which of the following items may be purchased with food stamps? (You may choose more than one answer.)
   a. diapers
   b. comet cleanser
   c. toothpaste
   d. cigarettes
   e. fried chicken from the deli

Answer: None of the above.

Source: U.S. Department of Agriculture (2009). This is a trick question. Nonfood items cannot be purchased with food stamps, thus eliminating diapers, cleansers, toothpaste, and cigarettes. The issue of fried chicken from a deli is a little confusing. Food stamps cannot be used to purchase food that can be eaten on site. For example, a person cannot go into a fast food restaurant and order a fried chicken plate and pay with food stamps. However, some grocery stores have delicatessens, so the food purchased there, although it is prepared, is occasionally covered by food stamps. There seems to be no universal application of qualification in this instance.

7. What was the average monthly payment a typical Supplemental Security Income (SSI) recipient received in 2010?
    a. $674
    b. $773
    c. $942
Note: The Social Security Administration provides SSI payments to residents who are disabled and therefore unable to work.
Answer: a.
Source: Social Security Administration (2010). If a grandmother is raising grandchildren and does not have legal custody of them, the only money in that household might be the grandmother's SSI check.

8. What was the percentage of U.S. households that had low food security in 2008?
    a. 5.7%
    b. 8.9%
    c. 14.6%
Note: Low food security means that one or more people in the household were hungry during the course of the year because the family could not afford enough food.
Answer: c.
Source: U.S. Department of Agriculture, Economic Research Service (2008).

9. What is the direct and indirect cost of substandard housing on children in North Carolina?
    a. $11.8 million
    b. $47.3 million
    c. $94.8 million
Answer: c.
Source: Chenoweth (2007).

10. What was the percentage of U.S. children who lived below the
    poverty level in 2009?
    a. 9.3%
    b 21%
    c. 27.3%
Answer: b.
Source: National Center for Children in Poverty (2010).

11. How is poverty measured?
    a. By determining the amount of money needed to buy the
       lowest-cost nutritionally adequate diet identified by the U.S.
       Department of Agriculture and multiplying by 3
    b. By estimating the amount of money needed to provide basic
       housing, clothing, food, and utilities, adjusted by the consumer
       price index, and accounting for the number of people in the
       family
Answer: a.
Source: U.S. Department of Agriculture (2008).

12. The elderly poverty rate in the United States is higher than the
    child poverty rate.
    a. True
    b. False
Answer: b.
Sources: U.S. Census Bureau (2010) and National Poverty Center
(2008). The percentage of Americans aged 65 and older was 12% in
2008, compared with 19% for children under the age of 18.

13. In 2004, U.S. taxpayers spent an unnecessary _____ to
    receive their tax refund faster through Refund Anticipation Loans.
    a. $7.4 million
    b. $1.24 billion
    c. $3.4 billion
Answer: b.
Source: National Consumer Law Center (2008).

You can also access information about poverty in your particular area at local colleges and universities, the United Way, and government offices. Now that you've looked at poverty statistics and have seen that poverty is something that is in our midst and affects us all, you might still think that those are just numbers and wonder what they have to do with your students. You might think that those numbers don't address the behaviors that you are struggling with in your classroom. This is why we must look beyond the numbers.

IS POVERTY A NUMBER?

According to the U.S. Federal Government, poverty is a number. As a single adult, you are considered to be poor if you have annual income of no more than $10,830. If you have a household with four members, you were considered poor in 2009 if your yearly income was no more than $22,050; therefore, if you earned $22,050.25 in a four-person household, you were not officially poor. This doesn't really define poverty. So what is poverty?

Poverty is the following:

- having no assurance that tomorrow will be even as good as today
- wondering who will be your friend today
- believing that hard work is hardly worth the little money you earn
- using other people's clothes, furniture, towels, and shampoo because you don't have any of your own
- having few dreams
- being invisible until "they" need someone to blame
- feeling frightened deep inside all the time
- being hungry at least one or two days a month
- walking everywhere, often for miles
- knowing that the doctor you see today will not be the same doctor you see next week
- laughing and crying when neither makes sense
- being consumed with the daily grind rather than the national scene
- not having toilet paper or even a functioning toilet

- having no bookcase because you have few, if any, books
- being angry, frustrated, anxious, and hopeless

DEFINING POVERTY

According to Charles Karelis, research professor of philosophy at George Washington University and author of *The Persistence of Poverty* (2007), poverty is, "Having insufficient resources to meet what are typically seen as basic needs in that place and time, whether those needs stem from our animal (physical) natures or not" (p. 3). Shakespeare's Juliet said, "What's in a name? That which we call a rose by any other name would smell as sweet." The way we talk about poverty directs the solutions we devise. Let's look at how our society often talks about hunger and notice how changing our own language can change how we view students and their families.

For example, Daniel Schorr once quipped that "hunger" is another name for poverty. When we talk about poverty as hunger rather than a complex of social and financial issues, we celebrate how we address hunger, for example, soup kitchens, food pantries, and free and reduced lunches at schools. We assure ourselves that we are successful when we quote numbers of hot meals served or food bags given.

We can also dismiss hunger, if we choose, by looking around at all the restaurants and grocery stores. We can comfort ourselves by proclaiming, "If there *are* hungry people here, then there are food stamps and all those soup kitchens and food pantries. No one is hungry here, and if they are, it is their own fault."

By naming poverty as only rumbling stomachs, we can avoid talking about the underlying reasons why hunger exists in our community. We don't have to address living wages and lack of affordable housing, public transportation to get to jobs, availability and affordability of quality child care and preschool education, and health care. Hunger is most certainly a subset of poverty. Unfortunately, poverty is bigger and deeper than hunger by itself.

Sometimes we lump our conversations about poverty under the term *welfare*. During his time in office, Richard Nixon moved from the language of opportunity that Lyndon Johnson's Equal Opportunity Act programs embraced to the language of "minorities" and "welfare." Poverty vocabulary moved from positive hope to negative exasperation. How we talk about welfare and poverty certainly affects our understanding of the issues, as well as the solutions we might propose.

POVERTY IS MORE THAN LACK OF MONEY

Poverty is more than lack of money. It becomes a way of thinking, reacting, and making decisions. As we move toward a deeper understanding of the issues that surround poverty, we will discover that there are significant differences between how you might view and approach the world compared with how a person who has lived in poverty might. This doesn't make one of you good and the other bad, it's just a difference in perspectives.

You will also discover that you share of lot of the insights that people who live in poverty have when you're willing to move beyond your presuppositions, prejudgments, and prejudices. As you learn more about the world of poverty, you will become more aligned with the needs of the children in your schools. We will all exceed our own expectations and those of our students when we deepen our understanding of poverty in the classroom. The numbers and descriptions provided in this chapter will begin to expand our understanding that poverty is real in our classrooms. But how does this really impact students? How does this hinder a child's sense of well-being?

③

SEEING WITH OTHER EYES

IF SHE WOULD JUST . . .

We want to help, we really do. We think we have solutions. If people would just do what we tell them to do, then life would be wonderful. We often say, "If she would just . . ." How many times has each of us said of a friend, family member, student's parent, or someone in the community, "If she would just leave him . . .," "If she would just get a job . . .," "If she would just take good care of her children . . .," or "If she would just try . . ."?[1] Our ignorance shows any time those words pop out of our mouths.

When we think, "If she would just leave him . . .," we are not recognizing that she may have inadequate education or no work skills with which to support her children. She may have no quality, safe, affordable child care to entrust her children to while she works or pursues further education. She may have no transportation to get to child care or her job. She may desperately want to work but doesn't have appropriate work clothes. She may have no one who can mentor her about how to get into the middle-class workforce. She may have no credit or bad credit and cannot get another place to live with utilities and a lease. She may be in a faith tradition that denounces her if she leaves. We are ignorant of the particulars of her situation.

When we think, "If she would just get a job . . .," our ignorance is self-evident in a slow economy. Even if she is fortunate enough to secure a job, the hours may be difficult for both her and her children. If she swings shifts, she has the issue of finding child care. She may work and still have no benefits. A sick child might cost her the hourly job she has. She may be promised 40 hours and then get 35 and then 20. She may not have enough time to deal with all the other issues of her children—schooling, health care, appointments, and so forth. She may ignore or ruin her health in trying to get by. Because she is female, she might not be paid as well as her male counterparts.

When we think, "If she would just take good care of her children . . .," we must remember that mothers may care for their children the way they were cared for; therefore, she may not have good parenting skills. On the other hand, she may know what she would like to do with her children but has no time to spend with them. Working and paying bills may consume all the time and energy she has. Stress may overwhelm even deeply caring mothers so they can focus only on survival, not nurture. Not having adequate resources means mothers must make decisions no mother should have to make, like "Do I feed the baby or my teenage son who is helping pay bills with his part-time job?"

When we think, "If she would just try . . .," we forget that women who work two or three jobs with hourly wages and no benefits probably work harder emotionally, physically, and mentally than many of us who are reading this book. After many unsuccessful attempts at change that failed for various reasons, she may wonder, "Why bother?" Feeling alone in her struggles, a woman may give up. She may have health or mental issues that limit her capacity to follow through with her plans. She may believe that her world can never be better than it is right now, so what's the use? When she begins to claim positive change in her life, her family and friends might make fun of her and call her uppity.

DRIVING TO THE MOON

It's easy for us to analyze others' lives and know what they should do. We think they should do what we would do. However, our plans are based on our own background, education, socioeconomic level, race or ethnicity, and family culture. What works for us might be destructive for someone else or as absurd as our telling them to drive to the moon.

Teachers really do want to help their students. They share stories of how they have reached out with good intentions. However, they acknowledge that at times they have felt taken advantage of. They may have been clueless about what to do. They may have gotten angry with the families they wanted to help.

In most instances, we really can help other people without feeling as if we've been duped. When we are willing, we can learn alternative ways to think about others' situations; develop unexpected solutions for long-held problems; and discover new avenues for success, interaction, and profound relationships. When you can better comprehend the students you want to help, when you are clear in your intentions for helping, and when you clarify for yourself what you will and will not do, you can offer significant and powerful assistance to the people you choose to care for.

WHY WON'T MY WAY WORK?

When we try to understand the situations of students who are living in poverty, we can reach out to them in more loving ways. When we are willing to set aside our own realities so that we can see the world through the eyes of the children we want to help, we are wiser and more compassionate.

Moving beyond our own ways of thinking and acting is challenging. We ask ourselves, "My way works for me, why won't it work for them?" It is important to remember that when we work with people who live in poverty, we need to put aside our value system, moral system, and decision-making process to be truly present for the people who come seeking our help. People who are from different socioeconomic situations, who are educated differently, or who are from a different race or culture do not always approach life, solutions, and situations the same way we do.

We understand this when we travel to other countries or even other ethnic neighborhoods in our area. We sense that our ways of thinking about things may make little sense to those whose environs we are visiting. People who are different from us in terms of race, socioeconomic status, or level of education challenge us to remove ourselves as the reference point for what should happen, how it should happen, and when it should happen, and that can be extremely difficult to do.

The easiest way to remove ourselves as the reference point is to assume a person native to, say, Beijing, China, is visiting. (This, of course, works only if you are not Chinese.) We would not expect her to have the same value system, have the same moral system, or make decisions the same way we do, because she is from a different culture. The same is true of the children we want to assist. The cultural difference may be socioeconomic, racial/ethnic, or related to education. One of us might be from a family that functions in a relatively healthy manner, while another is from a family that functions in a less healthy fashion. Whatever the specifics, we are reaching across a cultural divide.

Just as a Chinese person might use English words differently from the way we use them, people without resources use certain words differently from the way people with resources use those same words. For example, consider the word *time*. Those of us with resources can think in long blocks of time. We can think about vacations set to happen in a few months. We can think about retirement. People without resources think about time differently. For example, we might ask someone, "How long did you keep your last job?" The person may reply, "I kept it a long time." Our response might then be, "How long was that?" They might answer, "Oh, two months."

Two months for people with resources is not a long time at all, but when you have resources, you have no concerns about a roof over your head, food on your table, health care for your children, and other amenities often taken for granted in our culture. If you have experienced the loss of electricity during an ice storm, for example, you can begin to relate. Four nights and five days without power seem like a much longer time than four nights and five days with power.

Another word is *money*. Many of us with resources understand the word *money* to mean security. It means home, food, health care, and a retirement plan. To those without resources, the word *money* means more than food on the table or resources with which to pay the rent. It means "having the good life." This is why a teacher might do a home visit and find a gigantic television in the room. It may have been installed with a ten-dollars-down/ten-dollars-a-week plan. The television provides entertainment. It explains why a child might be on free or reduced lunch at school and still have an MP3 player. Money means having the good life.

DOUBLE STANDARDS

When we begin to think about techniques we can use to ensure that we are helping and not hurting, we also need to consider the double standards that influence our desire to help. We can't help but look at the world through our own lenses. We approach solutions to issues of poverty based on our gender, educational level, geographic area, age, socioeconomic status, and health. We tend to see faults and failures of another person without realizing that we, too, may be guilty of those same things. For example, we may get angry when people won't go to budgeting class to improve their financial situation, yet we don't go to the gym despite knowing that we need to exercise regularly to improve our health.

We both know what we need to do, but neither of us does what is necessary. The specifics of our "shortcomings" may be different, but the issues are the same. (We are not paying attention to our health—financial or physical.) We have double standards. To use a metaphor from the Bible, we see the speck in our neighbor's eye and cannot see the log in our own.

Let's look at a few of the double standards we have when we look at people who are poor and compare them to our own situations. As you consider these points, are there any that anger you, any that are a discovery to you, or any that closely fit the way you think?

Double Standard 1: "Poor People Who Stay Home with Their Children Are Lazy. I Applaud My Friends Who Stay Home with Their Children Because They Provide Consistent, Loving, and Quality Child Care."

Some government assistance programs require that the recipient work in the community (these requirements vary by state). However, when requirements for work are yoked with receiving financial assistance, child care becomes a challenge. There are not enough child care subsidies to go around. Child care is often expensive or, if affordable, may be of poor quality. When a mother who lives in poverty chooses to stay home with her young children, we often label her as being lazy. When someone we know in our socioeconomic class chooses to stay home, we applaud her for her commitment to her family or commend her for being so involved with her children. This is a double standard.

Double Standard 2: "People Should Not Need Government Services. So What if I Use Parks, Public School Systems, and Transportation Services?"

Government services that benefit people who live in poverty are often targets for cuts by legislators. The people who are most affected by these sometimes draconian measures are the least likely to be active constituents or voters. However, we all receive government services, either directly through our jobs (public school teachers, as one example), or we use public parks, airports, and so forth. When people talk about cutting government services, they are usually talking about the services that benefit "those people." We challenge anyone to touch the services that benefit "me and mine."

One service benefiting "me and mine" is the ability to write off from our taxes the interest we pay on our mortgages. Government-supported housing continues to be in a downward trend. (For ongoing updates about what is happening in low-income housing, visit www.nlihc.org, the website of the National Low Income Housing Coalition.) There is no community in this nation where an individual earning minimum wage can adequately afford a rental unit at the fair market rate. However, those of us who have mortgages on our homes receive a tremendous indirect governmental subsidy, a "tax break," when we deduct our mortgage interest on our federal income taxes. According to the Congressional Budget Office, the tax breaks for mortgage interests totaled $79 billion in 2010 (Rexrode 2008). The double standard becomes apparent when we realize that the government subsidizes mansions, yet safe and affordable housing is still a huge need in our country.

Double Standard 3: "Poor People Should Only Spend Their Money on Necessities, but Splurging or Treating Myself Is Okay Because I Deserve It."

For people who cannot meet their basic needs, it is very rational that one of the most important assets in their lives is the people and relationships they have. Some of the relationships are so intense that someone will even go to jail for a buddy. The other bottom line value is "having the good life." That, too, makes sense when you think about struggling day after day just for basic survival. When the opportunity for something nice comes along, you go for it. You know you might not have money next week, but right now you've got the cash, and you have a chance to be like everyone else and "have the good life." Entertainment can be a relatively inexpensive way to escape from the stresses of financial hardship. When money becomes available, spending it on entertainment may be a priority. Who doesn't want a treat after being deprived for a time?

A former colleague grew up financially poor. She said that at one time she owed the utility company money. She couldn't remember the exact amount of the bill but guessed that it was about $100. She called the power company and told them that she had $50 to pay on her bill. They responded that they needed $100. She told them that she didn't have $100 but that she did have $50 that she was willing to give them. They said they needed the bill paid in full. She asked again for them to take the $50, but they wouldn't take it, so she took the $50 and bought herself some new clothes. She tried to give them the money, but when they refused to take it, she treated herself.

Double Standard 4: "If People Would Stay in School, They Would Succeed. I Did!"

Staying in school enhances but does not guarantee success. A direct aid program paid the bill to reconnect electricity for a teacher with a master's degree. That same program assisted in restoring water services to a home where both adults had college educations. Former attorneys have lost everything due to drugs or mental illness. Nevertheless, we all know that education does improve our choices and options.

Today teachers are not necessarily the same race or from the same culture or socioeconomic group as their students. As important as racial differences are, the more important difference is socioeconomic. We absorb our vocabulary and values from our socioeconomic class. We learn subtle, and not so subtle, ways of thinking and behaving from our socioeconomic class.

Many teachers are middle class. They are challenged by students in their classrooms who come from poverty. For example, students who live in overcrowded situations may be afraid of silence. In their world, quiet often means that something uncomfortable or scary is about to happen. On the other hand, teachers require quiet in the classroom for desk work. Once teachers learn that their pupils may be unable to concentrate on their work when the room is silent, they can design ways to reduce the child's anxiety. They may play soft music, for example.

Double Standard 5: "If Poor People Would Leave Their Families, Get New Friends, Move from Their Bad Neighborhoods, Learn New Patterns of Thinking, and Develop New Ways of Relating to Others, Then Their Lives Could Improve."

Some years ago, I created a program for women who were homeless, pregnant, prostitutes, or suffering from an addiction. I and several committed volunteers met with the women weekly to discuss a variety of issues, including relationships, health, men, addiction, children, and other personal issues. We formed close relationships with the women and eventually became the women's best friends, and at the same time their worst enemies.

We gave kicks in the rear end or hugs as needed. Some of the women began to change their lives significantly. We helped them enroll in addiction and/or mental health treatment programs, find legitimate employment, obtain prenatal care if they were pregnant, and adopt new ways of thinking. As we learned more and more about their stories, we realized that some of the women needed to separate themselves from their families (since certain family members were their drug dealers or pimps), move from their bad neighborhoods (where drugs and violence were prevalent), learn new patterns of thinking (each person is valuable), and develop new ways of relating to others (foul language and bad attitudes seldom get you what you want). These tasks were huge, and yet some of the women were able to make the bold changes required.

When I realized what we were asking of these women and others in the various programs in the organization, I acknowledged the astounding fact that people were indeed changing their lives, even when faced with unbelievable obstacles. I recognized that I myself might not be able to do all of the tasks required for the kind of life changes they were working toward.

Are you willing to leave your family? Can you move from your neighborhood, where everything is familiar? Do you want to learn new patterns of thinking? Have you ever tried to break just one habit? Are you able to develop new ways of relating to others? These tasks can seem insurmountable and yet are often essential for redirection to happen. No wonder permanent change can be difficult.

Double Standard 6: "Those People Choose Their Lives. Sure They May Have Grown up in a Bad Environment, but That's No Excuse. I Pulled Myself Up. They Can, Too."

The family environment in which we grow up affects the options we have available in our lives. Most of us reading this book can choose where we prefer to live, which doctor we want to go to, where we want to shop, and what kind of car we prefer to drive. We are not forced to live where the rent is lowest or to use whichever health clinic has a doctor on duty. We do not have to shop at stores that are within walking distance, even though their products are of poor quality and have high prices because of the captive clientele of people who live in the immediate vicinity.

One donor truly believed that because he had overcome his childhood situation, anyone could. One day he came to my office, handed me a check, and said that he didn't understand why I help these people. I was genuinely puzzled by this comment, since he had just made a substantial contribution. I asked him to sit down so we could talk. I discovered that he was a self-made man and supported many charities. He had grown up on a farm and was the first in his family to graduate from high school and make his way in the world. He felt that if he could do it, anyone can. I thanked him profusely for his gift, and he left.

I continued to consider his assertion that if he can do it, anyone can. If I could have another conversation with that man, I would explain that growing up on a farm taught him the valuable lesson of cause and effect. He learned that if he wanted to harvest, he had to plow and plant crops. Many of the people I've worked with have not had the opportunity to learn about cause and effect. Then I would provide an example. Suppose one morning a child gets up and goes into the kitchen, where Mom hugs and kisses the child and tells him that he is the cutest child and how much she loves him. Then the next morning, the child gets up, walks into the kitchen, and Mom hits the child on the head so hard that the child slams into the wall. The following morning, the child gets up, goes into the kitchen, and *if* Mom is there, she totally ignores him. If that is the kind of environment you grow up in, you may not understand cause and effect.

If a child does not understand cause and effect, success in school may be difficult. Success on the job may also be challenging, because the employee does not understand that she cannot tell the boss that a certain task is not in her job description and keep the job. The family we're born into does make a difference in how we view the world, in the lessons we learn, and in the skills we develop for successful and healthy lives. Our family of origin affects the choices we have, as well as the quantity and quality of our decisions.

Double Standard 7: "Anyone Can Get a Job if They Want One. Of course, I Do Have Transportation, Child Care, Contacts in the Community, Adequate People Skills, and Good Health."

When people say, "Anybody could get a job if they wanted one," they usually follow with something such as, "I would flip hamburgers if my family needed me to do that." This comment indicates the person speaking has little regard for "hamburger flipping" jobs and thinks those jobs are demeaning. While "hamburger flipping" jobs are typically low paying, without benefits, and inconsistent in terms of scheduling, they are important jobs when a person needs immediate income or has a bad work history or no work history. "Hamburger flipping" jobs simply help a person stay in their current situation. Such jobs generally do not help a person progress to the next level.

Many people who work at "hamburger flipping" jobs do so to survive. They want more but have barriers to overcome. Getting and keeping a job is more than simply having a strong desire to work. One also needs the infrastructure of transportation, people skills, adequate health, and child care in order to be employed. We also know that there must be jobs available. Oftentimes, there are few jobs even for those with vast work experience and the required infrastructure for employment.

Now that we've considered some of the double standards that are alive and well in our society, let's consider what it might be like to not have all the advantages that we enjoy. Try the following exercise.

HELPING AGENCY XYZ APPLICATION[2]

We as a society often ask people (or parents of our students) to do what they cannot do. They cannot read. They do not understand our words. They have no framework for grasping what we are saying or explaining. When asked a question, they answer with what they think we're looking for so that we will like them and their children. They believe that by doing so, we will help them. However, their answers may not provide the information we need.

This exercise (see figure 3.1) allows us to experience the frustration of not being able to do something important when requested to do so because of a lack of understanding. Before looking at the application, imagine that you are applying for services at Helping Agency XYZ. You must answer each question or you will not be eligible to receive any services. Furthermore, even if you answer every question, if the interviewer doesn't like one of your answers, or if he or she discovers that you have lied on the application, you will not receive services at Helping Agency XYZ or anywhere in the community.

Praenomen:

Cognomen:

Address:

1. Were you ever rusticated?   Yes   No

2. Have you ever had to miss work due to the following?
      Accouchement?   Yes   No
      Contagion?   Yes   No

3. Would you describe yourself as being any of the following?
      Vituperative?   Yes   No
      Assiduous?   Yes   No
      Acrimonious?   Yes   No

4. Have you ever been accused of any of the following?
      Peculation?   Yes   No
      Catachresis?   Yes   No

Figure 3.1. Helping Agency XYZ Application

Of course this is not a real application, but if it were a real application, how would you have handled it? You might have asked for help, but this response requires a certain level of self-esteem. Many people will not admit they cannot do what you have asked them to do. You might have made an excuse, such as you forgot that you have an appointment and that you can bring the application back tomorrow once you have had time to fill it out. This might allow you to have someone else complete the application for you. You might have just circled the answers randomly, hoping that you selected the correct answers, just as you might have done on a test for which you were ill prepared. Or you might have gotten an attitude and stormed out of the room, since fear of being found inadequate can produce anger, a strong defense mechanism.

Applying the Exercise

This exercise is especially helpful to remember during parent-teacher conferences. A teacher may make a suggestion to a parent about how to help her child improve at school. The parent may nod and affirm that she will reinforce the suggestion. In reality, she did not understand what the teacher was saying, but she wants the teacher to like her and her child. The teacher believes that real communication has just happened and then gets frustrated later when the parent does not follow through. The mother was not trying to be difficult. She simply did not understand.

In a direct aid program, an older white male volunteer was interviewing an older African American female who needed help paying a bill. The volunteer asked the woman a question, and she answered. However, her reply did not quite make sense to the volunteer, so he repeated the question in a slightly different format. The woman answered again but still did not give the volunteer the response he needed to make a decision about assisting her. The volunteer excused himself from the interview and went to the manager of the program, a young African American female. He explained his situation, and the manager offered to talk with the lady. The manager asked the question a third time, and the woman answered again. The volunteer said, "That's not the same answer you gave me." The lady replied, "That's not what you asked me."

Was the difficulty communicating based on race, gender, or age? Who knows? The volunteer heard the same question asked three times. The lady heard at least two different questions. Being sensitive to the subtleties of communication and never assuming that the other person understands exactly what you said or meant helps open the door for compassion, deeper listening, and ultimately more authentic communication.

By experiencing the challenges of this exercise, you now have a better sense of what parents who are talking with you about their child may feel. You can be patient and understanding as you ask a question and pose the question in a variety of ways because you realize that the adult is not deliberately being contrary. She simply does not under-stand what you are asking. She wants to make you happy by giving you the answers you want. She is not trying to lie. She wants to help and be agreeable for her child's sake. When you remember the frustration you have felt when trying to do something you could not do, you can make a connection so you can reach out with love and care.

We have begun to look deeper into the world of poverty. We have considered how our own viewpoints are ours and are not universal. We have looked at double standards and experienced being asked to do something that we could not easily do. Now we will dig deeper into the world of poverty so we can understand the realities of students in that situation.

NOTES

1. The illustrations in this chapter are all female since female-headed house-holds tend to have fewer resources, as a whole.

2. Adapted from the *Adult Basic Skills Instructor Training Manual* by Whit-field, Parker, and Childress, 1992.

(4)

BECOMING AWARE OF
ASSUMPTIONS

FUNDS OF KNOWLEDGE

Different socioeconomic groups can have different bottom line values. Families who have lived in poverty for more than one generation often value relationships and "having the good life." This is rational behavior because when you do not have the resources to meet your basic needs, people become the most necessary aspect of your life. Through the people in your life, you find stability, a sense that you will survive no matter what happens, and your sense of worth. When you cannot meet your basic financial needs, having someone there is valuable.

Likewise, when you work multiple shifts each day just to get by, having the good life is enticing. Knowing that you can come home to a working big screen television can help you get through the day. Children watch television because they are not allowed to go outside in their unsafe neighborhoods while their parents are at work. When there is something you want, you know you'd better buy it today when you have money, because you might not have any money next week.

Middle-class people tend to value work and achievement. People in the highest socioeconomic class may value the networks they have and knowing who can help them close a deal or provide an opportunity for them. Some wealthy students choose the university they will attend based on who their peers will be for future help with opening doors to success and excellence.

We learn from the family in which we grow up. Our extended family—our "tribe," our culture—teaches us things that we do not even know we know. Because we simply absorb this knowledge, we assume that everyone thinks the way we do. We believe that our truth is universal, that it applies to everyone. Researchers Luis Moll, Cathy Amanti, Deborah Neff, and Norma Gonzalez capture this kind of knowing with the term *funds of knowledge*, which they define as the "historically accumulated and culturally developed bodies of knowledge and skills essential for household or individual functioning and well-being" (2001, p. 133).

Each socioeconomic group and each family has funds of knowledge, collections of truths, and understandings about how the world works. These funds may be distinct or varied. They are neither good nor bad, just different. For example, someone who has long lived in poverty may know how to live without electricity or how to barter for services. Someone from the middle class will likely know how to use the banking system and how to register for college and continuing education classes. Someone who is wealthy may know how to secure restaurant and hotel reservations around the world. People of color share a fund of knowledge that people with light skin do not have. Men's fund of knowledge is somewhat different from women's. Older people share a fund of knowledge that younger people do not have, and vice versa.

Because we tend to believe that our experiences are universal, we forget that our truth and funds of knowledge are not the same as those of someone else. We often suppose that we deeply understand what someone who is living in poverty is going through. The exercise on p. 37 will help expand your understanding.

Did you gain any insights from the exercise? Did you realize that although you may have used a Laundromat for six months as a college student or struggling young adult, this was not your long-term reality? Did you think about people who do this on a regular basis for years? If you have used a Laundromat in your life, you know about collecting your dirty laundry, carting it to the Laundromat, staying with your wash so it would not get stolen, and how much it costs to do several loads of laundry. How does this affect your ideas about what someone else should do? Are you able to be more compassionate about what they "ought to do"?

CHECKING ASSUMPTIONS

Place a check in each box that describes an experience similar to one you have shared.

- ❑ Spent the night in the home of someone who had significantly less money than you.
- ❑ Been without transportation to get to an appointment.
- ❑ Seen a different doctor every time you need medical care.
- ❑ Lived with only five books in your house.
- ❑ Asked your child to be the primary cook for at least a month.
- ❑ Lived with at least three generations in the same house.
- ❑ Washed your family's clothes in a public Laundromat for at least six months.
- ❑ Been unable to play sports because of financial requirements.
- ❑ Worked for minimum wage.
- ❑ Used a rent-to-own television.
- ❑ Lived without electricity for more than 18 hours.
- ❑ Had only one coat.
- ❑ Used a check cashing business.
- ❑ Been the only person of your race in a meeting.
- ❑ Had a family member with a life-threatening disease.
- ❑ Had only one bathroom in your house.
- ❑ Eaten the last two cans of food in your pantry.
- ❑ Taken a ride on a public bus.
- ❑ Not seen a dentist for at least three years.
- ❑ Had all your possessions thrown out on the roadside.
- ❑ Received financial help from your church.
- ❑ Shared a bedroom with more than one person.
- ❑ Been without food for at least 36 hours.
- ❑ Been watched closely while shopping.
- ❑ Lived for more than six months without health insurance.
- ❑ Been asked to move from your home.
- ❑ Moved at least three times in one year.
- ❑ Seen someone die.
- ❑ Walked everywhere you needed to go for a week.
- ❑ Worked three jobs at the same time.
- ❑ Had a car that was at least nine years old.
- ❑ Never been more than 10 miles out of town.

❑ Known someone who doesn't speak English.
❑ Been arrested by mistake.
❑ Avoided a bill collector.
❑ Had a family member with a drug or alcohol problem.

❑ Known someone who was not born in the United States.
❑ Lost a job.
❑ Smelled of kerosene.
❑ Placed buckets in your house to catch rain from the leaky roof.

When a group of graduate students did this exercise, one of the women asked, "In this box that says 'Seen someone die,' do you mean have I seen someone killed or have I been with someone who died?" I replied, "It doesn't matter. Have you ever seen someone die?" She rolled her eyes and looked at me as if I had just grown extra ears. She said, "Well, of course I've seen someone die." She looked around the room expecting to see all her classmates affirm her stance. She was shocked that only half the class had shared that experience. She explained that in her family they gathered at the bedside of a dying relative to ease their loved one's journey from this world to the next. This was what they did. Her reaction was a wonderful example of how we assume that our knowledge, experiences, and expectations are the same for everyone.

The more we can put our own assumptions aside and connect with one another, the more powerful our relationships can be and the more authentic the learning and teaching can be. Being able to affirm the experiences of the children in your classroom and their parents' knowledge can help build bridges and partnerships between the school and the child's community.

When you are willing to suspend your own convictions that your way is the right way or the best way, when you're willing to listen with interest and delight, and when you're willing to be taught by other people who have different funds of knowledge than you do, your life can be enlarged and you can help expand the lives of others. As you learn to listen with an open mind and welcoming heart, you take major steps toward building the deep relationships that are the key to the success of students in your classrooms.

$$\textbf{(5)}$$

DEEPENING OUR UNDERSTANDING

INADEQUATE HOUSING AND POOR NEIGHBORHOODS

While you can be aware that poverty exists, until you see it with your own eyes, you might have trouble accepting it as a reality where you live. One of the best ways to see poverty is to take a bus tour of blighted areas in your community. Arrange to ride the bus routes of the students in your school. If this is not possible, create your own tour. (See appendix A to learn how to set up a poverty tour.)

If you have never been to the neighborhoods where your students live, ask the school bus driver to allow you to ride along on the route. The bus routes that the students take to and from school each day provide a ready-made window into the world of children. Bus drivers are full of information about students in the classrooms, for instance, where they live, which family members they live with, when they live with those relatives or friends, and which children are fully prepared for a day at school and which are not.

Ask school administrators to arrange a tour of the neighborhoods for the staff and faculty on a teacher workday when the students are not in class and the buses are available. Teachers have openly acknowledged that seeing where their students lived has profoundly impacted their understanding of their students' situations.

A SCHOOL BUS TOUR

As you begin your tour, someone might suggest that she feels as if she is going through a "zoo" and that she is embarrassed. That is a valid feeling and one worth considering. However, until you have seen what is going on in your own community, you are less likely to feel compelled to do anything about it. Hiding behind your embarrassment does not help you become motivated to change how you perceive the young people in your classrooms, the same children who are living in poverty in the neighborhoods you see on the bus route.

As you are touring the area, listen carefully to the insights that the driver shares. He or she knows more about the lives of your students outside the classroom than you ever will. Pay attention in other ways, too. Do you see paths into wooded areas or bamboo thickets? Is there evidence of human habitation, for example, clothing, "roofs" made of cardboard or tarpaulins, cans, bottles, and so forth? You might look for evidence under shrubs near buildings. Look under bridges. Do you see signs of human habitation, for instance, sleeping bags, clothing, and so on? If so, some of your students may be living there.

Do you see satellite dishes outside apartments or buildings? If so, remember from our previous discussion that entertainment can relieve stress and anxiety, and also that immigrants, especially those who come from Spanish-speaking countries, like to keep up with news from home and view programs in their own language.

Do you see dilapidated houses with nice cars parked in front? It is helpful to know that it is *much* easier to get a car loan than a house loan. Most people might not know where someone lives, but they will notice the car they drive to work, to church, or to visit relatives.

Do you see houses with tiny rooms attached to the rear? These add-on rooms may be bathrooms that were required when outdoor plumbing was discontinued by governmental ordinances. In some communities, the building codes required that city water be run to the house, not *into* the house, just *to* the house. The people in the house might not have had the resources to connect the water. The landlord might not have chosen to attach the water. Many of the add-on bathrooms have only a toilet and a sink, and they may or may not be connected to the water and/or sewer system. A number of these connected bathrooms originally had a door that opened only to the outside of the house, because people were used to going outside to use the latrine.

If you see wooden pallets piled in a yard, assume that this is firewood. Some locales do not require landlords to furnish heat. The ordinance might stipulate that if the unit has a heat source, it must be functional. No heat means that residents are required to heat with wood being burned in a fireplace (wooden pallets that are used for firewood are made from pine, which is high in creosote and liable to cause chimney fires), or the family heats with kerosene (which leaves a distinctive odor on their clothing). Have you noticed that students in your class make fun of or say unkind things to children who smell of kerosene? If so, you might gently remind the class that smelling of kerosene means that no one froze to death last night.

Do you see boarded up houses? People may live in them, even though there is no electricity or water. Notice whether the boards covering the doorways are actually nailed or simply leaning against the door. Boards may be kept loose to allow residents to get inside. Occasionally, the windows will be boarded up and the door will be standing wide open. Abandoned buildings often provide shelter for people who have no-where else to go.

Pay attention to what is different about these low-income neigh-borhoods. In addition to the houses being small, old, and in a state of disrepair, streets may lack sidewalks, gutters, lighting, or driveways. Trash may be piled on the side of the street. Roads may be extremely narrow. What is missing from this neighborhood? Are there discrep-ancies between where you live and where your students live? Does this neighborhood feel safe for children and youth? Why or why not? What are the future implications for the children raised in these con-ditions?

MOTEL LIVING

The faculty of one elementary school took a bus tour of the neighbor-hoods where some of their students lived. The bus driver drove to an area with several motels. She announced that she stopped at each motel because children who attended the school lived there. That comment produced significant conversation.

Have you ever wondered why someone might live in a motel room when the cost for the month can be more than a month's rent in an apartment? If you think about it, the decision is extremely practical and rational for the following reasons:

1. There are no first and last month deposits required.
2. There are no utility deposits.
3. Cable television is often furnished.
4. There is hot water.
5. There is heat and air conditioning.
6. Furniture, sheets, and towels are provided.
7. There is no criminal background check.
8. There is no credit check.
9. You can pay by the day or week, which is extremely important when that is how you are paid.

Although the arrangements might be a bit crowded and cooking a little more challenging, all in all, a motel room is a pretty good option.

After you've seen where your students live, you will better understand that some kids come to school with odd smells on their clothing because they heat their homes with kerosene oil or there is no Laundromat close by. (Having a washer and dryer in the house is rare in these neighborhoods.) You will be able to grasp why some students seem tired all the time because of the gang or criminal activity on their street. You will know that loud noises in the night—either inside or outside of the house—do not support adequate sleep.

On the flip side, some students who live along the bus route have too much energy. Their mothers may instruct them to stay inside and lock the door until she gets home from work. Because of safety concerns, those children may have no playtime outdoors. Recess becomes a necessity for them, not a luxury or reward. You will also marvel at how some of your students are doing wonderfully with their lessons and becoming model scholars, even in the midst of their living conditions.

THE IMPACT OF SUBSTANDARD HOUSING ON CHILDREN

A study released in 2007 by David Chenoweth of Chenoweth and Associates, Inc., entitled "The Economic Cost of Substandard Housing Conditions among North Carolina Children," uncovered the high health costs related to substandard housing. The study examined the impact of environmental risk factors on the health of North Carolina children living in substandard housing.

Chenoweth and colleagues studied incidences of birth defects, unintentional injuries, lead poisoning, and cancer, as well as such neural behavioral conditions as autism and cerebral palsy, and such respiratory illnesses as asthma and acute bronchitis. They found that the "conservative estimate of total costs due to substandard housing-attributable childhood illnesses, injuries, diseases, and disabilities among North Carolina children is nearly $95 million" (p. 4).

We often do not think about housing as being a reason for why a child may or may not succeed in school. After seeing some of the neighborhoods, you realize that the amount of income that a family has affects the kinds of neighborhoods they can choose to live in. The neighborhood affects the kind of housing available. The amount of income and the characteristics of the neighborhood affect the parents' well-being, and all of that affects the child's well-being.

Recognizing how all of these factors tie together is key in understanding the challenges faced by some of the families represented in your classroom. Housing conditions, family situations, and the stresses of poverty affect the children in your classroom. Now we will move a bit deeper into our exploration of the challenges of poverty. The following exercise will help us grasp how difficult moving out of poverty can be.

CATHY

This exercise is helpful in realizing that the downward spiral of poverty is difficult to overcome. There rarely is just one thing that can be done to better a family's situation. Getting through the "system" often requires assistance that may not be readily available. A person in need may not know where or how to access services—case management, for example—even in cases where such services are offered in the community. People who have never faced the challenges of poverty may not realize the intensity of those challenges or the seemingly insurmountable barriers to overcoming the challenges.

Meet Cathy, a young woman who needs your help. Cathy is a 26-year-old female who is four months pregnant. She was living with her boyfriend in a small trailer until he physically abused her and threw her out. The boyfriend became angry when he found out that Cathy was pregnant, and he suspected that he was not the father of the child. Cathy spent the next three nights staying with various friends. Then she stayed in several motels until her money ran out. She is now staying with a cousin who lives in government housing with her family of six. Cathy sleeps on a couch and is afraid that the housing manager will find out about her and evict the entire family.

Cathy's mother is dead, and she doesn't know where her father is. She has two other children who have been placed in foster care. The younger child tested positive for drugs at birth, so Cathy is currently on probation for giving birth to a "crack baby." Although Cathy has been drug free for the past two months, she is in violation of her probation because she has not been to her drug treatment class for the past month.

Cathy has never held a job for more than a few months and has no marketable skills, but she does have a high school diploma. She has never had a driver's license, and her boyfriend flushed the contents of her wallet down the toilet when he threw her out. Cathy has been emotionally and sexually abused her entire life. She has low self-esteem, lacks self-confidence, and sees no way out of her trouble.

What would you do to help Cathy? You must decide how best to help her overcome the obstacles in her life. By helping her, you'll get a glimpse of how difficult living in poverty can be. Prioritize the following list of items that Cathy may need in her efforts to move toward self-sufficiency, number 1 being the most important, and number 19 being the least important.

___ counseling	___ employment
___ medical care	___ temporary shelter
___ clothing	___ legal aid
___ spiritual guidance	___ addiction treatment
___ furniture	___ identification papers
___ child care	___ permanent housing
___ transportation	___ utility deposit
___ probation meetings	___ rent deposit
___ mailing address	___ food stamps
___ job training	

After you have wrestled with the process, consider your priorities. Why did you choose the first three things on your list?

The following is a suggested priority list based on the three inter-connecting tasks of survival, stabilization, and barrier removal:

- *Survival:* If someone can be helped, he or she must still be alive.
- *Stabilization:* If the situation is unstable, accessing the life-changing opportunities needed to succeed is difficult, if not impossible.
- *Barrier Removal:* If someone lacks transportation, funds for tuition, money management skills, health care, or child care, he or she must have help to overcome these barriers to have significant, substantive change in his or her life.

Priorities for Cathy

There is no right sequence for Cathy; however, certain issues must be addressed in clusters. The tasks may not come together in the suggested order because of timing issues, such regulations as a required document that is not yet accessible, or availability of appointments.

Survival
- temporary shelter (night shelters, battered women's shelters)
- medical care (free medical clinics, community health centers, obstetrics clinics associated with hospitals)
- clothing (thrift stores, clothes closets, garage sales)

Stabilization
- transportation (public transportation, car rides by volunteers)
- food stamps (department of social/human services)
- mailing address (shelters for people who are homeless, general delivery at the post office)
- identification papers (highway departments for picture identification, social security cards through the Social Security Administration, birth certificates)
- job training (human service training programs, technical/community colleges, Goodwill)
- employment (state employment offices, human service organizations with job assistance programs)
- permanent housing (a job that will enable Cathy to pay cheap rent, sharing housing with another family)

Barrier Removal
- legal aid (to help regain custody of her children)
- Temporary Aid to Needy Families (TANF) (upon the birth of her child, Cathy may qualify for TANF assistance and subsidized housing)
- counseling (mental health centers, family counseling centers)
- spiritual guidance (church, other faith-based organizations)
- child care (state-offered vouchers, congregational based child care centers, human service centers)
- addiction treatment (drug treatment centers, Alcoholics Anonymous, in-patient treatment hospitals)

WHAT DOES THIS HAVE TO DO WITH ME?

You may be feeling as if the problems of poverty have little to do with you, except in the way they affect students in the classroom. You may still feel disconnected from the poverty in your community. It is important to understand that everyone is responsible for the existence of poverty and its ongoing reality in our midst, but we can also play a role in ending poverty.

You may feel if we keep trying to solve poverty with the same methods, tools, and approaches we have always used, we will never make a dent in the problem. We often feel bombarded by information, statistics, and predictions about the level and depth of suffering in our communities. So can we really eradicate poverty?

FIVE FACTORS

Dr. Phil Bartle (2010) has determined five main factors that promote poverty. These include ignorance, disease, apathy, dishonesty, and dependency. At first we might think that these factors apply only to people who are poor or not doing what we think they should do to help themselves, but they actually apply to all socioeconomic levels.

Ignorance

People with resources are often ignorant of the impact of poverty. They do not understand the tough decisions that poor people must make, and they are oblivious of the ways some of the structures of society make it harder for certain groups of people to thrive.

For example, have you thought about the profound ramifications of having an ineffective public transportation system? Suppose you had no car. Many communities have inadequate or completely lack public transportation systems. Imagine how your world would be different if after waking up, showering, and eating breakfast you walked out the door with no car. What time are you supposed to be at your destination? 9:00 a.m.? Oops, it is already 8:40 a.m. Does the bus come within several blocks of your home? How frequently does it come by?

Assume that you need to be at work by 9:00 a.m., that you have no car, that the bus stops two blocks down and one block over from your house, and that you must walk to the bus stop to catch the 7:20 a.m. bus. You will want to allow enough time to transfer downtown to the next bus that will take you to your destination. What if the bus is late? What if you miss the transfer? What if it is raining? What if your destination is a mile or so from the bus stop? What if? What if? These are decisions that must be made just to make it to a single destination. What about getting prescriptions filled? Going to buy groceries? Dropping your children off at child care?

When we take things for granted, such as reliable transportation, we are ignorant of how some of our neighbors live and the conditions with which they struggle. We consider how the parents of students are challenged by the barriers in their lives and then we search for ways to minimize those barriers so their children—your students—can succeed.

Disease

Being healthy is more than just being free of illness or disease. We already know that poor people suffer greatly because of inadequate access to medical care. Even when access is not a problem, paying for health care is prohibitive. A children's medical clinic in Boston has lawyers on staff to contact patients' landlords to instruct them to remove toxic substances and allergens from homes the people are living in. The result is that children with severe asthma—who had to stay on powerful medicines and miss many days of school—now attend class without the effects of potent steroidal drugs (Shipler, 2005).

In the documentary *Unnatural Causes: Is Inequality Making Us Sick?* (2008), producer Larry Adelman highlights the connections between health and socioeconomic levels. The work eloquently explains how high demand and low control lead to chronic stress, and how stress produces cortisol in the body, which leads to diabetes and heart disease. Segments inform viewers of the importance of one's street address in terms of good health, the impact of racism on such issues as premature births and low birth weights, and the effects of social policy. Adelman reinforces that poor health affects everyone and that it is part of the ongoing devastation caused by poverty.

Apathy

People who are poor or lack such resources as education or social contacts often feel powerless when trying to change their lives. It is easy to understand that if you've been beaten down by unkept promises, plans that didn't come together, people who let you down, or needs outstripping resources, then—as a pure survival strategy—you may stop caring. Apathy becomes a primary mode of getting through each day.

People with resources can be uncaring and numb to the realities of those living in poverty. We do not want to be inconvenienced or disturbed by acknowledging the pain in our broader communities. It is much easier to keep our blinders on and not confront the needs of those around us. If we don't know about a problem, how can we be expected to do something about it? Once you have taken a poverty tour in your community, it is impossible not to see the blight. Once you have paid a visit to a soup kitchen, you know that there are hungry people in your town.

When people do not care or have a feeling of powerlessness, they do not have the motivation to try to change things, right a wrong, fix a mistake, or improve conditions, but when they think they can help foster change, they do. A Russian proverb says, "Pray to God, but also continue to row to shore." Another saying goes, "We should not let God be used as an excuse to do nothing. This is as bad as a curse upon God. We must praise God and use our God-given talents."

Dishonesty

When you don't have adequate resources to meet your family's needs, you may be tempted to steal or lie just to survive. Through facilitating more than forty poverty simulations created by the Missouri Association for Community Action (2007) done for more than 1,500 people, we have learned about the patterns of coping that develop within the hour-and-a-half-long process. By week two of the simulation, someone in one of the families has usually begun criminal activities. The simulation allows for a volunteer to assume the role of illegal activities. We quickly realized that we did not need to fill that role because simulation participants inevitably began stealing from each other. Severe need tied with acute anxiety leads people to quickly revert to actions they never imagined they would do.

People who have resources can also be dishonest. However, this kind of dishonesty may be more subtle than stealing someone's television resource card in the poverty simulation. Dishonesty surfaces when people say they want to help and go on to demonstrate that they are not truly concerned about their fellow human beings by being too busy to volunteer, by writing a check that is only a pittance of what they could do, or by making caustic remarks about the people they professed to care about.

We are also dishonest when we believe that we are self-made people. We may talk of our relatively deprived childhoods and how we were able to pull ourselves up and better ourselves. We feel that if we could do it, anyone can. But we fail to ask ourselves crucial questions. Do I work with a computer in my profession? Did I create the software program(s) that I use to carry out my work? Did I develop the hardware? It is important to realize and remember that we stand on the shoulders of a lot of people.

Dependency

This is a dance that goes something like this: "I'm so poor and pitiful that you must take care of me. You or your ancestors or your political party did this, so now you owe me." The other side says, in effect, "You are so poor and pitiful that I must take care of you. You cannot take care of yourself." Even some of the rules and regulations of helping organizations have, in fact, encouraged dependencies.

When United Ministries of Greenville opened a day shelter for homeless people and washed clothes for an individual for six years without asking questions or providing any interventions for him, the shelter was inadvertently helping him remain homeless. The program had created the very behavior it was trying to eliminate. When the staff of the day shelter realized what they were doing, they changed their behavior.

Learning how we participate in poverty's continuing hold in our community is not to condemn us but to help us deepen our understanding of the issues. As we begin to focus on our own blind spots, we can do something about them. We do not have to allow ourselves to remain ignorant, apathetic, or dishonest. We can confront our own part in the dance of dependency and lack of focus on wellness and healthy communities. Now let's take a look at specific conditions and how they impact certain behaviors. We'll also discuss some suggestions for how to counterbalance the deterrents to a student's success in school.

II

HELPING STUDENTS WHO LIVE IN POVERTY

$$\textbf{6}$$

GRASPING THE EFFECTS OF POVERTY ON TEACHING AND LEARNING

Now that we have looked at some of the issues embedded in poverty, let's consider how specific details of poverty impact the success or lack thereof for both students and teachers. The social world of children who live in poverty is different from the social world of the classroom. Children realize at a very young age that the world is a diverse place, a fact that they may not appreciate and may actually resist or regret.

Knowing that they are "different" is not always a comfortable thought for anyone, especially children. Teachers who can appreciate the diversity in their students and help classmates be empathetic toward one another create environments that enhance and encourage learning by everyone, teachers and students alike.

When teachers become more aware of the realities that children living in poverty struggle with, they can access and incorporate the culture and funds of knowledge of all their students. They can use real-life lessons that the children can relate to and model acceptance and even celebrate the differences in pupils. They can create space for relationships and support for each other. By understanding certain behaviors that grow out of long-term poverty, teachers and school personnel can adapt their own behavior to benefit the children in their classes.

HIGH MOBILITY AND CONSTANT MOVING

Can you imagine what life would be like if you moved constantly? If your own parents were transferred for their job a lot when you were a child, you may relate to some of the disconnectedness students might feel. What *would* life be like if you never knew how long you might stay in one place? Would you feel that you had no roots, or would you become distrustful of what life had to offer? Would you be able to make friends knowing that you would eventually lose them? Or would you be overly eager in reaching out to others, maybe too aggressive in making friends, knowing that you had little time to spend with them? Would you be scared or timid? Or to the other extreme, would you be belligerent and haughty? Would you have trouble focusing on a single task or become easily frustrated? Would you feel that your life is out of your control? Would you feel safe in your surroundings?

What about school? Would you be upset about falling behind in your classes? Would you worry whether your school records would follow you from school to school? Would you be bothered by the fact that you have to leave a teacher you really like and who understood you? Do you ever think about what happened to your friends from your previous school? Do you wonder if your new school uses the same books? Do you worry about learning the new cafeteria routine? Do you even want to bother to do this one more time? When will you decide it's just not worth the effort?

When we try to see the world through the eyes of our students, we can learn measures we can take and plans we can implement to help. The following are some examples.

- Give a student something that belongs only to him or her. Having a plant to care for may provide stability in an otherwise unstable environment.
- Help students organize their book bags. If you find papers from the beginning of the year, be aware of the fact that they may keep them in their bag for a reason. For some students, the book bag and *all* of its contents might be the only thing in the whole world that they can call their own. Help them organize the papers from the entire year.

- Create a notebook for each student. At the end of each week, have students place work, goals achieved, and plans or tasks for the next week in the notebook. This becomes their personal progress record so they can reflect on their efforts and share them with a teacher or parent. Remember that the notebook should be about progress, not failure. (See appendix B for an example.)
- Assign a buddy to a new student. The buddy's task is to help explain the procedures of the school, for example, how bathroom breaks work, the procedure for recess, and so forth. For older students, a buddy can share which bathrooms to avoid, how to get to the cafeteria, where things are located in the classroom, and so on. Having a buddy provides a relationship for someone who feels isolated and scared.
- If you know that a child is leaving your classroom (although you often receive no notice of an impending departure), provide completed work papers and a good-bye card or note showing your appreciation for the child's presence in your life and classroom. This thoughtful act gives you both closure and helps provide a small bit of order in the child's life.
- When a child leaves your classroom, be sure to have a brief discussion about the event so remaining students do not feel confused or bewildered. They may also need closure for this loss to their small community. If age appropriate, ask students to write a note to their former classmate. They can share what they are doing in class, express that they miss their classmate or relay any other information that they feel is important. You can then mail the notes to the student if you know the new address. If you do not have access to the new address, writing the letters still provides the class with a sense of closure.

The important thing is to think what you can do to help children develop trust in a world that can be extremely unstable. How can you help them learn to make friends, be less aggressive, or focus on projects? What can you offer to a child who feels she has no control in her life? How can you help a child feel safe?

What ideas do you have for helping students who are new to your classroom? Do they need or want a buddy? What processes are in place for you to determine where their skill sets are? How can you help a timid child reach out? What can you do for a student in this situation who is angry? What have you and your colleagues already done that works with children who move around a lot? Once you better understand the impact of frequent relocations on children's lives, you can discover interesting and creative ways to help them thrive.

OVERCROWDED LIVING CONDITIONS

Some of us live in homes where each family member has his or her own bedroom and maybe even his or her own bathroom, but this is not the case for all families. Some families find that economic realities lead them to double up with friends and relatives. In some households, people come and go. Some cultures are comfortable with and even expect to have multiple families or acquaintances living together. Children may live in two-bedroom houses with eight other people and one bathroom. For some of your students, it may be normal to have numerous adults who may or may not be related, along with their children, eating, sleeping, and living in the house.

When a child lives in an overcrowded situation, he or she may learn to speak loudly to be heard. He or she may interrupt because breaks in the conversation rarely happen at home. If you do not understand this behavior, you may view the child as being belligerent or rude. However, this is not the case, as these are survival techniques at home.

The following are examples of things you can do to help children living in overcrowded conditions.

- Help children learn important contextual skills for the classroom by speaking in a soft, moderated voice and encouraging them to do the same. Remind them to wait for their turn to speak. Acknowledging that skills that are essential at home may be different from those appropriate for school means that you may be required to teach "double standards" of behavior (or what is known as "code switching" in multicultural education). For example, you want children to speak in "classroom voices" and not shout and holler, but you also know that being able to shout and holler may be an essential skill at home. You do not want children to interrupt you or their peers, yet they need to do this at home.

- Reinforce new behaviors by reminding students that when they are at school, there are certain rules that are in place that may be different from those at home. By doing this, you avoid forcing the child to choose between school and home. You affirm that both ways of behaving have their place and value in the life of the child.

- Give students a supply of sticky notes so that when they have a question or a comment, rather than interrupting, they can write it down on a sticky note. Provide a special location where students can place these notes during the day. Make it your goal to address by the end of the day each comment or question that has been posted. Adequately responding to the needs of each student will curb their vocal outbursts.

- If, on the other hand, a certain student is overly quiet, timid, and reclusive, these behaviors allow the child to avoid the chaos at home. This student, who is easy to overlook because he or she causes no trouble, needs your attention, affirmation, and guidance in significant ways. Find gentle connection points for this student. Be diligent about complimenting the student on a daily basis. The compliments do not have to be big, just genuine. For example, you might let him know that his smile brightens your day. You might tell her how much you appreciate how she organizes her work. Search for ways to help this child develop the confidence to speak up for himself or herself—at school.

- Play soft music (or music with a four-four rhythm) in the background to help children relax as they complete their schoolwork. Children who live in overcrowded homes may be afraid of silence. Silence for them may mean the "quiet before the storm." When teachers require silence while students complete desk work, some students may become anxious and unable to focus on the lesson. He or she may be paying a lot of attention, but not to the assignment. He or she may be watching to see what the teacher is doing and wondering whether a fight is about to erupt or something physical is about to happen. Teachers who understand this anxiety can provide relief by permitting a small amount of background noise in the classroom.

- Be willing to rearrange some students' schedules if the need arises. Students who live with many people may be tired and listless because the noise level in their homes at night might keep them awake. Even if they are able to sleep, they may not be getting deep and restorative rest. Children who live in homes where adults fight all night can't possibly come to school ready to learn. One teacher noticed that a particular student could not stay awake in the class. After exploring the situation a bit, he arranged for the child's schedule to be adapted so that the pupil could go to the health room for first period to sleep. Once that change was implemented, the child began to thrive.

- Pay close attention to students who appear to be disconnected from what is going on around them in the classroom. Children may have learned to ignore everything around them. They've developed this skill so that they can pretend that as long as they don't acknowledge any of the dysfunction in their lives, they are safe. When this behavior transfers to the classroom, the child may tune out everything and everyone. An astute teacher will gently ask the student to reconnect. If you notice that a student has stopped listening and taking notes and appears to have a blank look on her face, pull her back into what you are teaching by asking what she thinks about the topic being discussed.

- Be aware of students' personal boundaries. Children who live in overcrowded situations may have issues with people getting "in their space." One pupil may be perceived as invading another pupil's comfort zone when he or she is standing just inches away. This can cause feelings of anxiety for the student with personal boundary issues. Conversely, other students may seek extensive boundaries. He may not want to sit close to anyone. Do your best to accommodate these students. This might mean rearranging desks in creative ways.

- Encourage children who appear helpless to do things for themselves. If a child lives in a house with several adults and older youths, he or she may have learned helplessness. Someone is always there to step in and take over. For example, if the child is trying to cook, an adult may lose patience with the child's messy attempts and take over. This occurs mainly because adults who are stressed themselves may be impatient.

- Work to help a child who is quiet or depressed claim (or reclaim) his or her self-esteem. Unthoughtful adults may demean those around them, especially children. Children may receive constant put-downs, irritated retorts, and frustrated name-calling. Helping a child build self-esteem is a powerful building block for successful education. Find ways to help children excel in school, even if it is something as simple as giving them special jobs like asking them to collect papers or commending them for being the quickest to settle into their desks.

- Find creative ways to help students who are struggling with completing their homework. Homework becomes an issue for children who live in overcrowded situations. They may have no place to actually do the work. They may not have a quiet corner or kitchen table or adequate lighting to complete the task. Turn large cardboard boxes into homework desks that the student can use at home. Some schools use early and late bus time as homework time and station teachers in the cafeteria to assist children with assignments, if needed. You can also start signing the child's papers if the parents do not routinely take care of that responsibility.

As you think about the home situations of some of your students, you may be able to identify other behaviors linked to living in overcrowded situations. You may be able to discover other ways to help children overcome the barriers that their living situations create. Consult your peers and members of your teaching team for other ideas so that you and your students can succeed and thrive.

LACK OF ACCESS TO BASIC RESOURCES

How would you feel if you knew that your clothes were inadequate or different from those worn by your classmates? What behaviors might you exhibit if you were hungry? How would you act differently if while at school you had to worry whether your mom was able to avoid eviction or the disconnection of your electricity? What would your life be like if you couldn't get the reading glasses you needed, the corrective surgery that was simple yet essential, or the medication to keep your chronic illness under control? What difference would it make if you had no car to get to the store, to church, or to visit your friends?

How would you like it if kids made fun of you because of the way your hair was cut, the shoes you wore, or the way you smelled? How would you feel if you knew that you couldn't ask your mom for the fee for the field trip because she was already doing the best she could and not even three dollars was in the budget? What would happen if you knew you could not play sports because you didn't have transportation home after practice and couldn't afford uniforms, travel for away games?

All of this negatively impacts the school experience for students in your classroom. Some will welcome intervention and assistance for basic needs. Others will resent your help because they hoped you hadn't noticed that they were lacking. Disseminating information to parents can be challenging, but children and youth need access to basic resources.

The following are examples of things you can do to help children get the basic resources they need to get involved in activities.

- Encourage your school to sponsor an information fair with local organizations displaying the services they provide. Ask students to volunteer to sing or perform to get parents to come. Provide food and entertainment to make it a fun event. There are likely many resources within your community that can help parents that they know nothing about. An information fair is a great way for them to learn.

- Keep your students' situations confidential. We have all slipped up at one time or another, perhaps by asking a student in front of other students if she needs a voucher. This places children in an embarrassing situation. Even if you keep a box of clothes in your class, singling out a student to look in the box can be embarrassing. One teacher decided to have a "swap box" available to all children. They could swap for anything they wanted. (Some parents may not appreciate this. A lost and found box serves the same purpose.) Another teacher brought in clothes and announced that her child had outgrown his outfit. She thought it would look good on a particular student.

- Refer your students to the school social worker or health room worker who knows the community resources and can make the appropriate referrals, if necessary. They also usually keep extra items in their offices for children who need them. If you work at a school where children who live in poverty are in the minority, this may be the better option.

- Arrange the first period so that if children are late, they do not miss out on essential knowledge so they can easily catch up. When families do not have a car and the community lacks adequate public transportation, children may be late. We know to accommodate for children who ride the school bus and are tardy, but we often forget to be as understanding when students are late because of other transportation issues. Tardiness is often not the child's fault (this is often true of younger children). Don't penalize the child for her parent's behavior.

- Keep nutritious snacks in your desk for your students, even if your school offers both breakfast and lunch. Some parents may not provide breakfast for their children or the funds for them to buy something for themselves. Note: some students will take advantage of your generosity, so you need discernment for handing out snacks.

- Take the time to consider how certain situations may make your students feel bad. Even our best intentions can hurt kids' feelings. When some mothers bring in cupcakes for their child's birthday, other children who know that their mother will never do this may feel rejected or neglected. Some teachers have one party each month to celebrate the birthdays for all children in the class born during that month. Another school decided to provide backboards for science projects to all students rather than ask pupils to ask for a board if they needed one.

- Come up with creative ways to help families living in poverty over the holiday season. One teacher was seeking advice on how to do just this. Even though the majority of the children in her school came from financially stable families, there were about fifteen kids that the staff and PTA wanted to help. The group had collected a significant amount of money that they wanted the parents to use to purchase gifts for their children. The teacher needed ideas about how best to distribute the money. She realized that giving the parents cash might result in the money being used in ways other than those the school staff intended. She acknowledged that some of the families likely received special holiday assistance from helping agencies. The group did not want to assume parental duties and buy presents for the children, because they wanted parents to have this pleasure and opportunity. After consultation, the teacher decided that the best option would be to pay the rent or utility bill that month for each family. That meant the money collected by the staff and PTA was used in a way consistent with their desire to help, and the family would truly benefit. Parents could then use, if they chose to do so, the money they would have spent on rent or utilities to buy presents for their families.

INADEQUATE HOUSING AND NEIGHBORHOODS

When we become more aware of the harsh environments that some students live in, we realize that we need to adjust our educational approaches so that they can thrive under our care and instruction. What has worked with some children will not work with everyone, because the society continues to change and evolve. Some children are growing up with challenges that many of us could not even imagine.

From your bus tour of the areas where the students in your classroom live, you have seen the housing conditions and neighborhoods firsthand that are impacting your teaching efforts and your students' efforts to learn. While you can certainly advocate for improved housing and revitalized neighborhoods in your community, you also need to find ways to neutralize the effects of poor housing.

The following are examples of things you can do to lessen the negative impact of substandard housing on your students.

- Encourage your school to develop programs to help with housing. A Flint, Michigan, school district decided to help students with housing needs to stop the "revolving door" of students entering one school only to leave it two months later because the family had to move yet again. As many as fifty percent of their students changed schools during the course of a year. In 2004, they began an experiment called the Genesee Scholars Program that targeted second graders. The centerpiece of the program was a $100-a-month housing subsidy for families paid to landlords who agreed not to raise the rent and to maintain the unit to building code. Families in the program also received case management through a state-offered program.

- The forty families enrolled in the experimental program moved less, and as third graders, the students scored higher on a statewide test (Eckholm, 2008). By directly addressing how housing negatively impacted the students and the school itself, the program offered a solution to a seemingly insurmountable problem. Without finding creative solutions to help students outside of the classroom, schools struggle with resulting behaviors inside the classroom.

- Ensure that your students get ample time for recess. Especially in the primary grades, it is essential that children are allotted time for physical activity. Children who live in unsafe neighborhoods may not have the opportunity to play outside. Trash lying around and overgrown vegetation create dangerous places for children to play. Long-neglected neighborhoods are havens for people who also have been long-neglected, including drug dealers, mentally unstable individuals, and people who feel that they have nothing to lose. Lack of public playgrounds, sidewalks, and street lighting means that children stay inside. School recess may be their only opportunity to develop gross motor skills and learn to cooperate with others. It may be their only chance to release the natural, unbounded energy of childhood. While taking away recess is a disciplinary measure available to teachers, use this corrective device only when other options have been exhausted.

- Allow students living in poor conditions to use the bathroom as needed without making a production and drawing attention to their need to do so. These children may need expanded access to bathrooms and hot water to take care of their basic needs.

- Find ways to alleviate the anxieties some students may have while in the classroom. When safety is an issue in the home, children are even more sensitive to safety issues at school. For example, while a student is taking a test or doing desk work, he or she may become very anxious when you walk around the classroom. Rather than focusing on their work, they might focus on your location and what you are doing. They may fear that someone will walk up from behind and hit them, push them, or threaten them. They have been surprised by violence at home and may expect that same behavior at school. Finding ways to lessen this hyper-alertness will help students reduce their anxiety.

- Be on the lookout for signs that children are acting out inappropriately in the classroom, and seek assistance from school personnel: counselors, social workers, or health-related professionals. The neighborhoods where children live may allow them to be exposed to certain unhealthy substances and behaviors. These children may have already used a variety of drugs, even as young elementary students. Older students often have ready access to illegal drugs. Children may have witnessed criminal activities, violence, and overt sexual activities, and they repeat what they see and hear.

  Just because you may be horrified by something a child says or how a child acts does not mean that the child is aware of the inappropriateness of the behavior. Be sensitive to the child's "innocence," even while seeking ways to intervene. If you see a child acting out sexually, realize that there is an issue that requires further investigation. Children may be experiencing sexual abuse or simply acting out what they witness in their neighborhood. Remember that this does not make a child a deviant, pervert, or pariah. Investigate to see what can be done to change the child's behaviors and report your suspicions to proper authorities mandated by the state.

GREAT EXPECTATIONS

A temptation you may face when learning more about the environments where the children in your classroom live is to make excuses for them and expect less from them. This is exactly what you do not want to do. Your task is to help these children overcome the additional challenges they face because of poverty. You are not serving children well if you do not open doors for them so that they can excel and work to their full potential.

One of the highest compliments that a K–4 kindergarten teacher received was that all the K–5 teachers could tell a huge difference in the children she taught. They noticed the children's calmness, their ability to focus and complete tasks, and their teamwork skills. She understood what the children in her classroom needed to thrive. All teachers have the ability to develop those insights and skills. Don't make excuses for students. Expect great things.

(7)

FACING MORE CHALLENGES

Students who come from homes that lack adequate supports for learning come to school with significant challenges for overcoming the achievement gap. This perceived disadvantage does not provide the teacher an excuse for poor performance. A student once actually said, "What hurts us most is that you teach us less." Teachers are as challenged as their students to discover ways to fill the void of lean learning environments. Both teachers and students want to succeed. Understanding more about the effects of poverty helps breach that gap of lost opportunities.

FEAR

Educators know that understanding poverty in the classroom is central to the success and accomplishment of a vast number of students in public schools. Any good Internet search opens worlds of understanding that help spark our imaginations as we consider how we can improve our own interactions with children and help them reach their full potential.

One thing that research has discovered is that the most prevalent emotion for children living in poverty is fear (Pellino, 2007). What would your life be if you lived every minute of every day in fear? For example, are you fully engaged in the world around you? Do you embrace change and opportunity? Are you healthy? How about your attitude toward others? Are you belligerent? Docile? Open in your outlook? Closed? What about your energy level? Is it high or low? Are you always tired? How do you feel about yourself? Good or bad? Do you feel like you are in control of your life? If not, do you fight for control or acquiesce to whatever comes your way? What about your temper? With the increased levels of cortisol in your body because of the constant fear-induced alertness, are you angry? Are you reactive?

As you think about how pervasive fear affects a child's ability to learn and engage in school, you begin to realize some of the things that schools can do to reduce fear in students, including the following:

- Create a safe haven for students. We know it is easier to decide to do something than to actually accomplish it. When a student goes on a shooting rampage, when a child kills herself after being the target of school bullies, or when a significant drug bust goes down, we realize that safety is often elusive. Creating safety in schools is not simply a matter of adding more security guards or locked doors (although this is necessary at times). Safety involves a school design that fosters positive energy and excitement for learning.
- Creating a safe environment involves providing nurturing and meaningful relationships with all students so that they have alternatives to violence in dealing with their frustrations or anger. Some teachers stand at the door and greet each student by name. They may "high five" them or mention a team or performer if they know the student is a fan.
- Invest time and energy in improving and maintaining the appearance of your classroom and school. The appearance of a school sets the tone for learning. Schools that display students' work, have signs written in the language(s) of all the students, and are brightly lit or painted indicate that they are places for learning, motivation, and enthusiasm for education.

  Two different elementary schools are demographically comparable in terms of their student body, but their environmental differences are remarkable. One school has soft, comforting lighting in the office area. The area is decorated with lamps, comfortable chairs, and green plants that creates a family room feel. The other school has harsh overhead florescent lighting and furniture that looks institutional, at best.

The first school makes it easy for parents and visitors to sign in because the computerized sign-in area is at waist level, and a staff member is present to help if someone is unfamiliar with the process. The second school has the sign-in computer at shoulder height, and even someone who frequently works with computers has difficulty figuring out how to sign in.

In the media center of the first school, all the displays are positioned at a height where children can comfortably view them. The displays at the second school are all up high, near the ceiling, so that no one can touch them. Which school do you think creates positive energy and excitement for learning?

- Demonstrate that you are available to students outside of class. Teachers who attend the occasional ball game, concert, play, and other events where students can see them show just how much they care. Special relationships can be nurtured by agreeing to be the sponsor of a school organization. Being available before or after school so students can "drop in" to talk when they are ready is important. As any parent knows, you have to make yourself available so that when your children are ready to talk, you are ready to listen. They certainly do not talk with you according to your schedule.

- Focus on being relevant to students from all cultures so that they feel a strong sense of belonging and ownership to what happens in school on a daily basis. Hans Schmidt, a second-career teacher who was raised and educated in Germany, attended one of my workshops. He was teaching in a low-income high school. When I asked him his subject, he said, with his very German accent, "I teach Spanish." My immediate reaction was that he was kidding, but he confirmed that he indeed taught Spanish.

During the course of the workshop, he shared that he had been put on a teacher improvement plan because the administrators and students thought that he lacked rapport and that he was aloof. He admitted that after looking up the meaning of those words, he was totally surprised. He thought he was a good teacher because he was teaching as he had been taught in Germany. He was doing what came natural to him. He failed to realize that American teachers were more informal and interactive with their students than his teachers in Germany had been. He had not adapted to the culture of his students.

Understand that cultural differences are significant components of creating safety for teaching and learning. The German teacher who teaches Spanish is learning that building relationships and valuing each student for his or her uniqueness, skills, and talents enhances learning and reduces anxiety.

• Be knowledgable about the many ways in which you can encourage students to express and process their feelings. Schools and school districts have professionals who are trained in counseling. Health officials can also be great resources. In some communities, congregations or corporations "adopt" schools, thereby providing resources, needed supplies, willing volunteers, and trained personnel who can reach out to students. Other schools have older adults who volunteer and become surrogate grandparents. Certain nonprofits partner with schools to get students involved in programs designed specially for youth. Learn about the options in your community so you can get your students the help they need.

• Embrace the uniqueness of each child and find ways to help each one flourish. Celebrating differences while also finding commonalities creates safe zones for learning and reduces fear. Everyone wants to feel accepted. We want to be treated fairly and acknowledged. When someone calls us by name, we feel acknowledged. When someone remembers the names of our family, what our favorite color is, or what we love and hate about school, we feel seen. When someone compliments us on how we handled a challenging task, even if we didn't do it perfectly, we feel important. Students need to know that someone cares, and in a good way.

• Show that you take pride in and have enthusiasm for your job. Safety is enhanced when all school personnel commit to having a positive attitude about their profession, the work they do, and the impact they have on the lives of others. Negative comments, feelings, and actions reinforce fear and lack of safety. When you visit an organization and you see that all of the staff love their jobs and are proud of the work they are doing, you know it is a special place.

What might happen if that kind of enthusiasm and pride was voiced regularly in all the schools in our country?

- Maintain a relaxed atmosphere in the classroom. Students' fear is lessened when the learning environment is relatively stress free and perceived threats are minimal. Curricula that are culturally relevant and emotionally connected and that use various methods of presenting lessons enhance learning and reduce fear.

EFFECTS ON STUDENT ACHIEVEMENT

When some parents play with their children, they instinctively insert lessons into the play. For example, a mother may say, "Please give me the purple ball," rather than "Give me the ball." Her child now has an experience with "purple" as well as "ball." Or a dad may count the steps as he and his daughter climb to the second floor of their home. Some parents know how to open their children to learning.

Unfortunately, some parents do not know how to embrace learning. They never experienced that joy for themselves, or they don't have the energy or time, so they think, to help their children learn. If parents had an unpleasant experience with school, their attitude may affect their children's outlook toward school. If parents repeatedly received the direct or indirect message that they were stupid, slow, or a failure, they may convey the same message to their children.

The following are a few ways that teachers can inoculate students from some of these negative messages.

- Encourage positive outcomes, cheer students on in their endeavors, and model nurturing relationships. Teachers can help students feel good about themselves, and every child has some trait that deserves positive acknowledgment.
- Work with your school administrators to provide curricula that are strenuous and challenging but that also allow students to enjoy their success. When students conquer lessons that stretch their capabilities, they realize they can climb mountains. Conversely, if a child continues to get watered down schoolwork or the same lessons year after year, the inadvertent message sent is that you don't

think they can do the more challenging work and that maybe one day they will finally master the lesson so that you can all move on.

In the early days of an adult education program at United Ministries, the staff ran into a limiting mind-set. The curriculum required that students master one lesson before moving on to the next. One segment that was particularly challenging focused on the grammatical constructs of gerunds and participles. Students could not get their minds around these concepts, which for them were unusual. Some even dropped out because they got so frustrated.

One of the staff members finally looked at the GED exam to see how damaging it would be if students never understood gerunds. As it turned out, there was only one question that related to that topic. After further research, the staff decided to have students try the lesson, but if they did not understand it, they could move on. The adult education students did not lose their confidence in their learning and capabilities because of a lesson that was ultimately inconsequential.

- Work with your teaching team to design creative ways to keep children involved without getting overwhelmed by areas of weakness. One school administrator once said with disgust that children should not be halted in their math progress by requiring them to go over and over their multiplication tables until they have mastered that skill. She felt that it is best to keep moving ahead, while also circling back to work on the tables. Go ahead and introduce simple algebra or other math challenges. Don't wear children down with repetition so that they totally disengage from the math process.

- Include lessons that are relevant to your students' lives to keep them involved. A teacher once wanted to learn more about the cultures of the students in her classroom, so she visited a student's home (Moll, Amanti, Neff, and Gonzalez, 2001). While there, she learned that her student knew how to work on cars because he spent Saturdays with his uncle, who was a mechanic. She also learned that the young boy had a small candy selling business on the side.

With that information, she returned to school and worked with the teaching team to develop an entire unit about candy. They used geography to teach where the ingredients used to make the candy came from. They used math to figure out profits and losses. Developing marketing materials required reading and writing skills. Students enhanced their interpersonal skills and cooperation as they worked together. Before she had expanded her appreciation of her pupil's fund of knowledge, she had only a limited view of the child. With her newfound understanding, she was able to connect in more authentic ways to enhance the learning of everyone in the class.

- Use written materials and real-life illustrations that students can relate to. If you need help, ask a parent to partner with you to find new ways of thinking and conceptualizing. By admitting that you have gaps in your own learning, you can have a greater appreciation for the knowledge held by those around you and expand your own learning. Your life will be enriched beyond your expectations, and your students will thrive because they are being taught by a teacher who understands their world.

- Listen for clues about what your students are interested in, the types of people they admire, and the issues that they struggle with. Try to incorporate similar instances into your lessons so you can make connections with the student's world.

1-2-3

Teaching children how to make choices when they feel that they have no control is an important life lesson, as well as a confidence booster. When a child asks for a pencil at home, he may be given one, yelled at, ignored, or even hit. The child may learn never to ask for anything at home because he is uncertain of the reaction he may get. And so the child learns not to ask for anything at school, either. An astute teacher will ask, "Do you want the yellow pencil or the green one?" letting the child know that he can have a pencil and that he can also decide which color he wants.

Children who have never lived in one place long enough to make plans for the following summer or the winter holidays may not be able to think long-term. Some of the children in your class do not live in an ordered world. Their world is one of chaos. Things do not always move in chronological order, 1-2-3. Take, for instance, the development of cause and effect that was discussed in chapter 3. When you live in chaos, you may not develop a grasp of cause and effect because your behavior reaps multiple effects. You never know what is going to happen when you walk into a room. Will you be ignored, hugged, scolded, or hit? Moving along a continuum is challenging because your world does not operate in such a way.

Some of us grew up in families that reinforced lessons about the progress of events. We learned that B follows A, one plus one equals two (in a decimal system), cooking by a recipe involves a logical progression, and that making a bed involves three easy steps. By the time we learned to write term papers, it made sense to make note cards first, then develop an outline, and finally write the paper. Even those of us who found parts of that process difficult knew how to adjust the process without getting derailed.

The following are a few methods teachers can use to help their students develop an understanding about the progress of events.

- Divide large tasks into smaller ones. Some students may need help in learning how to break projects into discrete steps. Explain the steps involved in completing a specific task. As students accomplish each step, affirm their progress and help them decide what their next move should be.
- Develop skills for sequential learning. Children will not walk into the classroom knowing how to organize material or how to progress in small steps that lead to large steps that lead to huge steps. Divide tasks into discrete elements to assist students in increasing their processing skills and have them evaluate their progress. Gradually add a few more elements and then a few more. Students will eventually learn how to do this for themselves with less and less guidance. Encourage students to partner up on occasion so they can learn to work together in completing a task.
- Teachers in the Carolina First Center for Excellence program in Greenville, South Carolina, use sticky notes when approaching a task that has many layers. Teachers instruct students to write one idea for how to reach their goal on a sticky note. If a student has three ideas, he or she should use three sticky notes. Then the class

(or a small group, depending on the class size) puts all the sticky notes in the middle of the table or on a board so that everyone can see them. The students then put the notes in categories of similar tasks. Next they rank the tasks within each category. At the end of the exercise, all the students have participated in developing a logical process for accomplishing the larger task. The students can then use the plan as a checklist to help them stay on task. If a student gets bogged down, the teacher knows exactly what to focus on and can assist the student in developing a solution to overcome the barrier.

- Develop methods to help students transition from one subject to another or from one activity to another. Students who live in uncertainty may not be able to recognize when the teacher moves from general conversation to a lesson or from one lesson to another. Teachers who are successful in helping students succeed develop rituals that cue their students that a lesson is about to begin. Just as the yellow traffic light lets us know that we need to prepare to stop our car, subtle signals can help students prepare to pay attention.

  For example, one way to indicate a transition is by moving from one place in the room to another specific location, like from the front of the desk or podium to beside a piece of equipment. You may ask a student for the page number on which the lesson begins. You may develop a funny hand signal that indicates that you are about to switch tasks. You may even have a musical ditty or silly poetic phrase that indicates that you are going to impart information. Find what works for you and your students.

- Use a variety of teaching methods to adapt to your students' various learning styles. Some children learn by hearing, others by seeing, and others by touching. Incorporate these various styles as much as possible so that all students can feel the wonder of learning. A child who needs to touch to learn may thrive by using a computer but have difficulty listening to a lecture. A child who learns by seeing will do better with written rather than oral instructions.

  Children from deprived educational home environments may have learned only by hearing, not seeing or touching. Or if the television is a child's only model for experiencing the world, the usual way of presenting material in a classroom may be slow, too involved, or dull. When the home environment does not tap into the child's natural learning style, helping the child discover new ways of accessing education may indeed open worlds for him or her.

- Be consistent, be consistent, be consistent. By modeling consistency and routinely adhering to rules, teachers demonstrate that the world can be safe, predictable, and secure. When a child feels safe and begins to experience a sense of control over his or her world, then the risks and challenges of learning become exciting rather than threatening. Schedules can be invaluable in helping a child develop the comfort of structure in his or her life.

RELATIONSHIPS

The importance of relationships to children who live in poverty cannot be stressed enough. They depend on relationships to anchor them in their uncertain world. Unfortunately, some of their relationships with people in their lives have not built them up but rather added layers of self-doubt, negativity, and a sense of failure.

Adults who point out a child's failures, mistakes, and shortcomings do not instill confidence in that child. When children are compared to family members who are not respected, the child assumes that he or she deserves no respect either. When children are verbally, emotionally, or physically attacked by adults in their lives, they either withdraw or fight back. They do not have the skills or the strength to deflect consistent put-downs and barbs. They learn to either trust blindly or not to trust at all. They crave attention or they learn to "disappear," even if they are still in the room. They may not know how to belong or make friends. They need relationships that are healthy, whole, and dependable, and that's what a teacher can provide.

The Gallup organization developed what they call Q12, a test that employers can give to their employees to determine whether the employee is engaged, not engaged, or actively disengaged (Thackray, 2010). (Interestingly enough, the findings indicate that three out of four employees are either not engaged or actively disengaged in their work.) It is important to note that some of the criteria measured by the test include whether employees receive adequate recognition or praise while at work, whether they feel that they have someone at work who cares about them, whether they feel encouraged as they perform their jobs, and whether they feel that their opinion is valued in the workplace. All of these criteria point to the value of relationships in achieving success.

The following are a few practices can teachers adopt to help build meaningful relationships with their students.

- Stand at the door to the classroom and greet students as they enter each morning. While in the classroom, work to let students know that you like them and that you are their advocate for helping them succeed in life and accomplish their goals. Without a process for reassuring students that you value your relationship with them, you will discover that students pay a lot of attention to you, but not to the lesson. Instead they are paying attention to your attitude. They are trying to figure out whether you like them before they feel comfortable listening to you teach.

  For example, an employee was very proud of the job he had because he had come from poverty and succeeded beyond his family's expectations. The work project he led had experienced significant growth, and he was no longer accomplishing the goals that the program required. His supervisor sat down with him and gave him a list of tasks that he needed him to accomplish. After hearing the list of requests, the first thing the employee said to his supervisor was, "Okay. But you still like me, don't you?" The supervisor replied, "Of course I still like you."

  After a couple of weeks, the supervisor went back to her employee and reiterated that his job performance was not what it needed to be. She reminded him again of all the duties he was responsible for carrying out. Once again he asked, "But you still like me, don't you?"

  The supervisor finally realized that she was going to have to dismiss him because the program needed more than he was giving. Had she fully realized the importance of relationships to the man, she admits that she would have begun every conversation by saying, "You know that I really like you. I want you to succeed here. But to do that, I need you to do this, and then I need you to do this, and then I need this." The supervisor learned after the encounter that until she assured him that she liked him, the employee could not hear anything else she said. The outcome might have been the same, but the employee would have been more likely to hear the suggested corrective actions because his supervisor had confirmed that she liked him before she made suggestions for improvement.

- Challenge students to reach for the stars, and support them in their journey. If they fall down, help them get back up. Cooperative learning processes can be a resource for addressing some of the needs of students who depend on strong and healthy relationships in their lives (Kagan and Kagan, 1994).

- Encourage good behavior in positive ways rather than with criticism. Some children are adept at dismissing criticism but crave positive interaction. East North Street Academy dedicated itself to discovering things students do that are positive rather than negative. Each time a teacher, administrator, volunteer, staff member, or even a student notices someone doing something good or something special, that pupil receives an "Excellence Dollar." These dollars can be used at the school store to purchase age-appropriate items.

- Encourage students to focus on the efforts they put forth to accomplish something and not the final outcome. Pretests and posttests can be helpful as students build on their skills. The pretest may demonstrate how little a student knows about or understands the topic. Following instruction about the topic, the next test may or may not show that the student learned something. If the student earns a D and then moves on to the next topic, no learning takes place. The information that was tested by the exam on which the student earned that D was quickly forgotten or was never learned to begin with.

On the other hand, when the first posttest identified that more learning was required for a student to grasp a concept, help the student and then test again. It is important to remember that errors are part of the learning process. Remember learning to ride a bicycle? By having opportunity to keep learning, the student experiences accomplishment, not failure. Give the student opportunities for improvement and do not accept poor performance.

- Work to improve the self-talk messages that students hear in their heads. Just changing "I am stupid" to "I can learn" can alter a child's entire world. Changing "I am bad" to "I have value" or "I can't do this" to "I can solve this problem" can make a huge difference. One teacher changed his student's self-talk in a way that became destructive to the student. When Mr. Ostrowski asked Malcolm Little what career he thought he'd like to pursue, Malcolm answered, "I've been thinking I'd like to be a lawyer" (Haley, 1965, p. 43). The teacher, thinking he was being kind, suggested that Malcolm develop more realistic dreams, for example, becoming a carpenter since he was good at working with his hands. Malcolm knew that he was smarter than most if not all of the other students in his class, but the teacher's comments planted seeds of deep discontent. Malcolm later changed his name to Malcolm X (Haley, 1965).

- Encourage children to dream big and help them figure out how to pursue those dreams. Treat students as active partners in the learning process and not simply as vessels into which you pour knowledge and information. Actively engage students in their own learning and provide a world of joy through learning so when the child returns to his home environment, he or she has more tactics for basic survival.

THE IMPORTANCE OF LANGUAGE

How we use the English language affects the power of our communication. The words and tone we choose can build people up or tear them down. The way we use language deeply affects the realities of life. (Many schools face additional challenges because of the different languages their students speak. Those challenges are beyond the scope of this book.)

All children need affirmation, some more than others. In "What It Takes to Make a Student," Paul Tough (2006) reports on a research project by Betty Hart and Todd R. Risley, child psychologists at the University of Kansas, who in 1995 published the results of an intensive research project on language acquisition. They discovered that by the age of three, children of parents working as professionals had heard 500,000 encouragements, whereas children of welfare parents had heard 75,000 by the same age. The children of parents working as professionals had 1,100-word vocabularies, whereas children living in poverty had 525. Discouraging remarks were 80,000 for professional families, as compared to 200,000 for welfare families.

What this research tells us is that our students need encouragement and affirmation. Some children need more than others because they have not been raised in environments that reinforce their worth, capabilities, creativity, and inquisitive natures.

The following are a few tips for using language to help your students grow.

- Choose your words wisely. How we talk and the words we choose affect our communication in powerful ways. The subtleties of our words can impact behavior, feelings, and outcomes. For example, have you ever thought about the difference between "I can't" and "I won't"? I learned this distinction when my sons were growing up. My older son wanted me to attend an open house at his school. Normally, I would have rearranged my schedule to be at the school, but at the time I felt that it was essential to be elsewhere that night. I committed to visiting my son's school and seeing his work the afternoon prior to the open house. However, this was not the desired outcome for my son.

  I tried to explain the importance of the meeting I had to attend and said, "I can't be at your open house, but I will come that afternoon." He retorted, "You could if you wanted to." I responded, "No, I can't." He countered, "Yes, you can." (This was not one of my finer mothering moments.) Then I said, "Son, I *won't* come to the open house. I will come in the afternoon." I was astounded when the argument stopped—immediately. That's when I learned the power of language and the words we choose.

  Another word difference that can be powerful is the difference between "but" and "and," two commonly used words. Note the difference: "Keisha, I think the concept for your paper is wonderful, but your grammar can use some improvement," or "Keisha, I think the concept for your paper is wonderful, and your grammar can use some improvement." The sentence that uses the word "and" rather than "but" sounds much more positive.

- Educated young parents now say "Good job" to their children when a child does something notable. Years ago, dedicated parents most commonly said, "Good boy," or "Good girl." By changing one word in the compliment, the parents changed the focus from personhood to action.

  Some teachers have moved beyond saying "Good job" to using even more powerful affirmations that link praise with specific skills demonstrated by their students. For example, when a child helps another child with a task, the teacher might say, "When you helped Marcus complete that task, you demonstrated cooperation and sharing. Good job," or "You have been practicing your math skills. I can tell by the way you are working those problems. Good job." These students are able to build their confidence and increase their competence because of regular affirmation from their teachers.

- Use humor in the classroom, but do so with caution. For example, you might say, trying to be humerous, "You're going to look funny with no head if you don't sit down at your desk immediately." Most children will know that the teacher is kidding around and that he or she is not going to cut off anyone's head, but some children, especially those who are living in the midst of domestic violence, may become terrified at what they perceive as threatened violence.

- Pay attention to the tone of your voice as you speak. Eric Berne (2010), a noted Canadian psychiatrist and best-selling author, highlights the three voices that we use in our verbal transactions with one another. He says that the "child voice" is emotional, whining, angry, or despairing. When we use our child voice, we might say such things as, "You can't make me," "You made me feel this way," or "I hate you." The "parent voice" is judgmental and patronizing. Favorite words of the parent voice are "always," "never," "should/could/ought," and "do/don't." When we use our parent voice, we might say such things as, "You know you shouldn't do that," "Because I said so," or "Do what I tell you." The "adult voice" is nonthreatening and straightforward. When we use our adult voice, we might say, "I see it this way, but you may have a different viewpoint" or "Help me understand."

While we like to think that we are mature and always use our adult voices, we must acknowledge that at times we use our parent or child voices. The adult voice is instructional and invitational and thus is the most beneficial to students. It is a voice that is typically calm and not anxious. When you slip into the parent voice (which is a tendency when you're the adult in a group of children), you close doors to student exploration and investigation. When you always tell children to do something a certain way, you discourage their inquisitiveness and eagerness to seek other options.

Avoid using the parent voice with children who are raising themselves. These kids are doing everything they can to hold their families together. Challenging their parental role by using the parent voice can destabilize the control they have established. Obviously the child voice is inappropriate for the classroom, which is full of children.

- Consider how formal, informal, and popular or colloquial English affect the classroom. Formal English tends to be precise and uses complete sentences. It uses proper grammar, and contractions are rarely used. Spoken words are pronounced correctly without dropping final consonants. Words, rather than motions, carry the story. Stories told in formal language are fairly straightforward and can be easily mapped for setting, characters, the problem, the plot and events, and the resolution. As teachers, we use mostly formal English in the classroom setting. But some students have not had this style of communication modeled for them outside of school.

Informal language is the language of everyday conversation. Speakers relax their grammar and pronunciation. They may not speak in complete sentences. Body and facial cues help carry the message. Storytelling is more circular than with formal English.

Popular or colloquial English is colorful and highly expressive, carried out with gestures, changes in voice pitch, and body movements. Grammar is not important in delivering the message. Some children hear only this style of language in their homes and communities. They can have a difficult time understanding formal English unless they are taught how to use and understand it.

The oral tradition of storytelling may be used by the families of some of your students. When asked to tell a story, they may not state that first this happened, then this happened, then this happened, and then the end. Instead, they will start at a point in the story that seems appropriate to them and weave the facts together. Oral tradition uses gestures and invitations to enter the story all along the way. The story does not simply entertain, although that is important. It pulls the listener into relationship with the speaker. This style of communication makes a lot of sense for people who value relationships over work and achievements.

Teachers can learn to appreciate the nuances of popular or informal speech while teaching formal language, the language needed for job interviews or higher education. The engaging aspects of oral tradition can be something that you value as you learn to connect with your students in amazing ways so that you can succeed as a teacher and the student can excel as a learner.

Expecting all students to know how to switch from formal to informal to colloquial English is unrealistic if they've never experienced the various ways of communicating. Even as students begin to learn about grammar, complete sentences, and correct pronunciation, they may be reluctant to use it and practice it if no one in their family speaks that way. They may feel that they are being disloyal to the people who love them and take care of them if they speak in a different way.

Sensitive teachers will realize that changing how one speaks may be threatening for some students. They will help students learn that different styles of language are appropriate for different situations. For example, when you hear a friend talking on the phone, you can often tell who they are talking with just by listening to their tone of voice, their facial expressions, and the inflections of their words. Likewise, talking at home may be different from talking with a teacher or principal. The challenge is learning to know when to use which speaking style. Effective communication means comprehension between the listener and the speaker.

Becoming aware of how living in poverty affects your students will help you adjust your teaching style to better meet their needs. Just as the German teacher teaching Spanish had to adjust his style of teaching, you, too, can make small changes to help your students reach their potential.

DEALING WITH OTHER STUDENTS' ATTITUDES

As a teacher, you can do everything suggested in this book and a whole lot more to help students who live in poverty thrive at school. However, even your best attempts can be undermined by negative or even ugly comments made by classmates. The following exercises are helpful in dealing with this.

TRADING PLACES

The purpose of this exercise is to help students empathize with classmates who live in poverty. By taking a closer look at their own situations, they can see what they have in common with people living in poverty, as well as the things they take for granted. This exercise is designed for teens who have resources. If the group is economically mixed, ask students to work alone and then volunteer to share their thoughts. Allow them to skip any question that they do not feel comfortable answering.

Ask students to form small groups. You may want to ensure that friends do not all group together. Have students count off, divide them up by birth dates or ages, or use some other system for forming groups.

Create a handout based on the following ten questions. Allow room for students to write their answers. Because you know your class, you know whether this will work best as an individual, small-group, or whole-class project. Remind students that they can skip any question that they feel uncomfortable answering.

After the students have completed the questions, allow them to share some of their answers. Do not require each person or group to share all of their answers. Review the questions from the perspective of having limited income.

The goal of the questions is to help expand your students' understanding and empathy.

1. What is your favorite music group? How many of their CDs or songs do you own?

Follow-up: People who live in poverty may not have the funds to purchase music by their favorite group. Sometimes, however, because entertainment is highly valued in lower income groups, they may have a sizable collection. On the other hand, when people move a lot, which happens often when a family cannot pay their rent, when the primary breadwinner leaves the home, or when someone is ill or has lost a job, whatever items one may have collected may have to be left behind. There may be no time to pack and move. The family starts over again in their next home.

2. Where are your favorite places to eat? How many times a month do you go to those restaurants?

Follow-up: Can a person who is poor afford to eat at those places? How do they get there if they have no car? If a person has only $1 to spend on a meal, where can he or she eat out? If a meal costs more than $1, then what does the person do for the other meals?

3. How many pairs of athletic shoes do you own?

Follow-up: Some people are lucky to own one pair of shoes. They may spend a lot of money to buy that one pair, but they plan on wearing them for an extensive period of time. A mother may buy her children expensive shoes to demonstrate her love, rather than thinking ahead about paying the water bill. In some communities and cultures, nice shoes are a status symbol and a sign of respect.

4. What sports do you play? Do you play on organized teams? Do your teams travel? Where do you go?

Follow-up: Being on an organized sports team is expensive. Uniforms cost money. There may be no way to get to games unless transportation is provided by the team. Going to tournaments costs money for lodging, food, and travel. Some families do not have extra money for these opportunities.

5. How is your home heated? Do you have a gas furnace, electric furnace, or a heat pump?

Follow-up: When building codes do not require that a home has a heat source, then the home will be cold. If there is no furnace, the family often heats the home with a wood-burning fireplace or kerosene heaters. Have any of your classmates ever smelled of wood or kerosene? If so, at least they were warm last night and didn't have to worry about freezing to death.

6. How many coats do you own?

Follow-up: Many students are lucky to have one coat that fits them.

7. Do you receive an allowance? How often? Are chores required for you to get your allowance?

Follow-up: Allowance. What's that? When a parent is working two or three jobs just to pay the rent and feed the family, there is no extra money for the children to have an allowance or money of their own. Some of your classmates may be doing all the cooking and caring for their younger brothers and sisters because they must help out their mom while she is at work. They don't get paid to do that, and they certainly don't receive an allowance.

8. How many times in the past year did your home have no electricity?

Follow-up: About the only time many of us lose electricity is when the weather is bad. We complain and view it as a major inconvenience. We rarely lose our power because our parents did not have enough money to pay the light bill. We may live in homes that have good insulation and windows that are energy efficient. Some families have to pay as much to heat their small, drafty homes as your parents pay for your larger home. If you had to live without electricity for two weeks, could you do it? How would you handle that?

9. Do you expect to attend college? Why?

Follow-up: College is typically not even an option or matter for discussion for families who live in poverty. No one in the family has ever attended college. It's too expensive.

10. What are your favorite stores for buying clothes?
Follow-up: Did anyone name a thrift store? Goodwill? A consignment store? Garage or yard sales? Can people without a car get to the stores you enjoy?

A BAG OF CHIPS

This exercise is for students of all ages. Its purpose is to help students understand that our lives are enriched by many other individuals in ways that we seldom think about. We rarely realize how dependent we are on people from all socioeconomic classes. By considering all of the people who are involved in producing something as small as a bag of potato chips, students can begin to realize how other people enrich their lives on a daily basis. This can help youth develop empathy for different types of people.

Place a bag of potato chips on a table in the middle of the room. Ask students to brainstorm and make a list of everyone who was involved in making the chips. Answers may include farmers, pickers, truckers, processors, and grocery store personnel. Then encourage the group to dig further. You may prompt them by asking them to think about the specific functions or jobs on the farm that are required for them to have a bag of chips. Don't forget the owner of the farm, the purchaser of seeds, the mechanic who keeps the equipment running, the field workers, the people who build the boxes and shipping containers, and so forth.

Keep pushing for more answers. The processing plant employs computer engineers, housekeepers to keep the plant clean, chemists to develop the chip recipes, human resources personnel to hire the workers, and so on. Beyond that, professors and students at universities explore ways to produce better potatoes. Graphic artists design the chip bag, and advertisers try to convince us that this bag of chips is better than another. There could be as many as 100 people involved in the production of a single bag of chips.

Discuss the importance of each person and whether each should be valued equally for their role in the production of the chips. Discuss the interconnectedness of people, our caring for each other, and how each person is important to our own personal enjoyment of life. Allow students to share their perspectives and suggest ways for improving how we appreciate and treat others.

JAR OF MARBLES

This exercise works well with elementary students. It serves as a reminder that many people are hungry and in need of food on a daily basis. Contact an organization in your community that gives out food bags or serves meals to people who live in poverty. Ask the organization how many people received food handouts the previous month. Fill a jar with that number of marbles. Ask students to guess the number of marbles in the jar. Depending on the guess, indicate whether the number is high or low. You may want to offer a prize to the person who guesses the correct number. Then talk about the marbles and what they represent. Help students understand that there are people in their community who are hungry and ask for suggestions about what they can do about the problem.

⑧

AND THEN THERE ARE
THE PARENTS

How many times have you heard someone say or even said yourself, "If the parents would just do what they're supposed to, then we wouldn't have any problems"? Parents can be a wonderful resource for the classroom or a huge impediment. Like it or not, you cannot ignore, blame, or dismiss the parents of your students.

In the poverty simulation developed by the Missouri Association for Community Action (2010), participants are required to keep their "families" housed, fed, and safe for a month (that is, for four 15-minute weeks). "Families" receive information about their demographics, income, and expenses. They negotiate with such "vendors" as pawn brokers, employers, schools, and mortgage brokers. After about an hour and a half, people often become angry, frustrated, and anxious. Then the participants debrief following the experience.

The people who participate in the simulation are usually educated community and congregational leaders, donors, and/or students. During the debriefing, participants often confess that they did things they thought they'd never do and share that they are surprised by their actions. They may have stolen from their "neighbors." Those who had a job in the simulation are horrified that they allowed their "children" to be unsupervised for significant periods of time. They acknowledge that there was just not enough time to get everything done. Others depended on their "13-year-old child" to take care of paying bills to the vendors. Some found it a relief to end up homeless because they no longer had to worry about keeping their family fed and housed. "Children" admitted that while they were in school, they spent their time wondering if "Mom" was going to get the bills paid. They were afraid that they might not have a home to return to after school let out.

Participants are likely to admit that they literally shake, their stomachs churn, and they feel stressed and anxious after dealing with their overwhelming challenges for an hour and a half or so. They talk about the people in their community who experience these issues on a daily basis.

For the parents of some of the students in your classroom, their life is more than a simulation. They work multiple jobs and still cannot earn enough to support their families. They escape from the grinding challenges that their situations present in unhealthy ways. Even when they do their best, it is rarely enough. They do what they can and model how they were raised. When they feel like a failure, they resent anyone who tells them what to do. They struggle, fall down, get up, and fall down again. They feel afraid, tired, and neglected. If you want to reach their children and engage the parents as partners in their child's education, you must first understand the parents.

Many teachers complain that parents don't care, that they don't love their children, and that they do not get involved in their child's education. School administrator Olivia Morris disagrees with teachers who feel that some parents enjoy a role of noninvolvement. She feels that if children come to school dressed and on time, the parents are involved. Getting their children to school dressed and before the first class begins may be all they can do, but doing so is huge.

Part of understanding poverty in the classroom is understanding how some parents may think based on their own experiences and backgrounds. For one parent-teacher conference, a mother brought her two-year-old child with her. The toddler stood by the mother's side the entire time, never saying a word, never fidgeting, and never engaging with the adults at all. The mother was proud of the way she had taught her child to behave. The teacher, however, was horrified at how unnatural the child's behavior was.

As we discussed the puzzling episode, I asked the teacher, "What message do you think this young mother received when she was growing up? She's obviously pleased with her parenting skills. So what message is she living into?" The teacher lit up and said, "Children should be seen and not heard." By realizing this, she was able to understand her student on a deeper level.

Was this young woman a bad parent? No. Could she benefit from some other messages about children and what is appropriate behavior? Yes. Would a compassionate teacher not judge this woman harshly but rather make positive suggestions, if appropriate? Yes. Could the student benefit because his mother and his teacher connected on a level deeper than discussing grades? Yes.

Occasionally, when you are interacting with parents, you have the opportunity to give them some prompts to help them learn how to enhance their child's learning. Below is a list of activities that parents can engage in. Consider making this list available as a resource at parent-teacher conferences, and be sure to commend any of these things that the parent already does. If they only do one or two things, encourage them to build on their success. You might want to post the list on your website. We all need new ideas for being better parents and partners in children's education. The list is not to be used to correct or judge parents. It is simply a tool for you to have available if a parent is eager to learn new ways to encourage his or her child's success in school.

HOW TO HELP YOUR CHILD SUCCEED IN SCHOOL

- I read to my child.
- I praise my child for good work.
- I display my child's schoolwork for others to see.
- I pay attention to what my child is watching on television.
- I discuss television shows with my child.
- I turn off the television when there are shows with violence in them.
- I talk with my child's teachers.
- I volunteer my time and talent to my child's school.

- I enjoy my child as we grow and learn together.
- I ask my child's teachers questions about my child's progress.
- I make sure my child attends school on a daily basis.
- I take an interest in my child's schoolwork and his or her test grades.
- I speak positively to my child about his or her teachers and counselors.
- I talk to my child about the benefits of education and the disadvantages of not having an education.
- I make sure my child gets to school on time.
- I attend open houses and parent-teacher conferences.
- I encourage reading and writing.
- I keep books, magazines, and newspapers in my home.
- I take my child to the library.
- I discuss what my child reads.
- I encourage my child to write notes to friends and family.
- I make sure that my child arrives at school well-rested.
- I set a regular time and find a quiet place for my child to do homework.
- I ask my child what he or she learned in school that day.
- I celebrate my child's successes.
- I look for things to do together as a family.
- I set fair and consistent rules for my child.
- I encourage my child to ask for help when he or she is uncertain about something.

Sometimes parents respond in ways that make little sense to us at first. What that actually means is that the parent has not responded as we wanted him or her to. One teacher spoke about a student who fought in class. She called the child's mother to report the incident. She expected the mom to say, "Don't worry, teacher. I'll have a talk with him. You won't have this kind of trouble again." Instead, what the teacher heard from the mother was, "Good, I've taught him to stand up for himself!" The teacher was frustrated and felt that she had received no support from the parent. She was ready to dismiss the entire family as hopeless.

As we talked, she began to realize that being able to defend oneself is a survival skill in some groups of people. She began to understand the mother's reaction. When the teacher called the mother to tell her about the fight, the mother did not hear a complaint; she heard the teacher compliment her child. The child could defend himself, and that was something to celebrate. The teacher realized that she still needed to help her student learn other ways of dealing with his frustration. Nevertheless, being able to defend himself was an important survival skill for this particular child.

Other teachers have told how frustrated they become when trying to get parents to sign papers that give permission for certain needed services to be provided for their pupils. Again, parents are living based on their own experiences. They may have had bad experiences in school. They may be afraid of or distrust of authority figures. They may not want to sign anything they do not understand because they fear their child will be taken away. Even when they understand that their child might benefit from additional services at school, they may believe that their ability to parent is in question because their child needs help. They will never allow themselves to be accused of being a "bad" parent.

It is important to remember that children should not be punished for not getting papers signed. We all know that some kids intentionally do not show their parents schoolwork for various reasons (primarily because they do not want to be fussed at). However, whether a parent ultimately signs a paper is out of the child's control. Children cannot make their parents do anything; therefore, they cannot be held responsible for their parents' actions. Understanding some of parents' fears and beliefs can help school personnel be more empathetic, establish trusting relationships, and help their students succeed.

STAFF MEETING WITH PARENTS

Let's imagine that the school faculty and staff want to learn more about how parents think and what their needs are to better connect families and the school. As part of the administration's research, the principal decides to invite certain parents to a meeting with the faculty. It is now

Wednesday afternoon, and some parents have agreed to meet with the staff. Let's eavesdrop on the meeting.

Parent 1

Administrator: Welcome. We understand that you are working two jobs and that it is very difficult for you to meet with us. Thank you. What we are trying to do is discover ways that we can better connect with parents. We all want what is best for your child. We see ourselves as partners with you in helping your child to be the very best that she can be. Would you please tell us a little about your life and how we can better work with you?

Parent: As you said, I work two jobs, so it is very difficult for me to come to meetings or conferences at the school.

Administrator: I understand. Do you have any ideas about how we can stay in contact in other ways?

Parent: Well, I'm free on some weekends. Do you ever have meetings then?

Administrator: We've never done that, but that doesn't mean that we can't. Do you ever look at your child's schoolwork when she brings it home?

Parent: She leaves it on the table sometimes, and I look at it then. If there's something she needs signed, she knows where to leave it so I'll find it.

Administrator: Occasionally, we need to contact a parent. Is one way better than another? Can you receive calls at work? Do you have access to e-mail?

Parent: I'm not allowed to take calls at work, except when I'm on break. I don't have e-mail.

Administrator: We hope this would never happen, but is there someone we can call if your child gets hurt at school?

Parent: I guess you can call my mother. You have her number.

Administrator: I can't imagine working two jobs and raising children. That must be incredibly challenging. Is there any way we can help you?

Parent: I like coming to programs when my daughter is performing. If I have enough notice I can sometimes switch my work schedule around.

And when you have dinner along with the program that really helps me because I don't have to think about feeding my kids on top of everything else.

Administrator: Those are great ideas. Sometimes we like for parents to help us with special projects around the school. I realize that with two jobs that might be difficult, but is there anything you might like to do?

Parent: I love to bake. If you can get me the ingredients, I can cook for you on the weekend. I'd really like to do that. I might be able to help out doing something else, but I have to have a lot of notice. And you have to ask me directly. I want to know that you want me to do something.

Administrator: Thank you so much. You've given us wonderful ideas. We really appreciate your being with us today. Here is my phone number in case you think of anything else.

Parent 2

Administrator: Welcome. We understand that you would like to volunteer but that you need more information. We hope this meeting can help answer questions for all of us. Thank you for coming. What we are trying to do is to discover ways that we can better connect with parents. We all want what is best for your child. We believe that we are partners with you in helping your children be the very best that they can be. Would you please tell us a little about your life and how we can better work with you?

Parent: I really love my children.

Administrator: I know you do. Do you have some free time? Perhaps you'd like to help out at school?

Parent: I have two mornings a week, but I don't know what to do. I came up here once to help with . . . I think it was the T-shirt sale . . . but I felt like I was in the way. All the other parents already knew each other. They didn't need me.

Administrator: That doesn't sound like fun.

Parent: One other time, I signed up to volunteer, but nobody ever called me. I figured that they didn't want me. Oh, there was one time, but I couldn't get here. I don't have a car, and so I have to get somebody to bring me.

Administrator: We haven't done a very good job, have we? What can we do now to be better partners for your children's well-being?

Parent: Do you ever have people from my neighborhood volunteer? Maybe I could ride with them. I'd really like to be here to help, but maybe someone could teach me what to do. You know those other people always dress so nice, so maybe that's why they don't want me.

Administrator: Sounds like we need to do a better job of helping our volunteers to get started. What do you think about us partnering you with another volunteer?

Parent: That might work. I want to be here. I just don't know what to do.

Administrator: After you learn a bit more about the school and the volunteer opportunities here, do you think you might want to help us connect with other parents, maybe some of those from your neighborhood?

Parent: Maybe. I love my kids. I want to help.

Administrator: Thank you for coming. This has been very helpful. Oh, by the way, how can we get in contact with you? Do you have a phone?

Parent: I do right now. You can always send something home with my child.

Administrator: Thanks again for coming. You've given us a lot to think about.

Parent 3

Note: This is not actually a parent but a child who is in charge at home.

Administrator: Thank you for meeting with us. I know this is kind of scary, meeting with all the teachers, but we're trying to understand how we can help all the kids in our schools. We know that you're very brave in deciding to talk with us. Is that okay?

Child: I guess so.

Administrator: Can you tell us a little about your life? How many brothers and sisters do you have?

Child: I have one brother and two sisters.

Administrator: What are their ages?

Child: My brother is 14, and my sisters are 7 and 4. I'm 9.

Administrator: And what about your mom?

Child: She's sick a lot. When she's there, she lies on the sofa most of the day.

Administrator: Does she cook for you?

Child: No, I do that.

Administrator: Does she help you with your homework?

Child: No. I help my sisters with theirs. My brother doesn't have homework. Anyway, he's usually not there.

Administrator: Who gets you up in the morning?

Child: I get us up, help my sisters get dressed, and then we go to the bus.

Administrator: What do you have for breakfast?

Child: We eat here at school.

Administrator: When we are on holiday at Christmas or in the summer, where do you eat?

Child: At home or at the community center or at the kitchen down the street or at Grandma's house.

Administrator: Who signs papers that the school sends home?

Child: I sign them for my sisters. Don't get us in trouble, okay?

Administrator: Okay. With all that you do for your family, what is school like for you?

Child: I'm tired a lot, but I love school. We eat here, and there's heat in the winter. My teachers are nice. I wish we could stay here all the time, but my mom needs me.

Administrator: I'm glad that you like school. You're doing a wonderful job here and at home. I'll make sure that your teachers know what a special person you are. Thank you for meeting with us.

Child: Okay. Can I go now?

These three scenarios are just a snapshot of what some of the families in your school are struggling with. Administrators and teachers who understand the realities of poverty can be more accommodating to the special needs these families bring forth. The following are some other ideas for connecting with and building trusting relationships with parents who live in poverty.

- Use a variety of ways to contact parents or guardians, including voicemail, e-mail, and flyers providing regular updates.
- Connect with a parent or grandparent who can convey information to the families living in their neighborhood.
- Hold meetings away from the school in your students' neighborhoods when possible.
- Always serve food and have children do some kind of presentation at important meetings.
- Provide parents with multiple ways that they can contact teachers or administrators.
- Provide a welcoming environment at the school so parents want to visit.
- Invite parents to eat lunch with their children.
- Be *REAL*:
  - *R*each Out. Invite parents to participate in their child's learning. Communicate according to the parents' schedules. E-mail, phone, write, or journal within the parents' time frame.
  - *E*ncourage. Empathize with parents. Thank them for everything, including getting their children to school on time.
  - *A*ccept. Know that all parents, regardless of their income, work situation, and so forth, care about their kids. Respect them accordingly.
  - *L*earn. Take time to learn about the family's needs and strengths.

A WORD ABOUT PTA MEETINGS

A school administrator had been to numerous PTA meetings as a professional educator. She always sat with other teachers at the meetings. She did not intermingle with the parents unless intermingling was on the agenda. She sat through the financial report to learn if she was going to receive any PTA funds for a special project she was working on. She hoped that the guest speaker, if there was one, would not be long-winded. She was tired and wanted to get home. She was always disturbed that so few parents were at the meeting, but after years of poor attendance, she had low expectations.

Then she married a man with several children, and she began attending PTA meetings as a parent. She was astounded that not a single educator sought her out to talk with her about her children. She had not had time to feed the kids prior to the meeting and the babysitter had fallen through, so she went to the meeting with hungry and tired children by her side. After all the effort she had put forth to attend the meeting (as an educator she knew how important attending the meetings was), she yawned through the financial report. She hoped that the speaker would give her some good ideas that she could use as a parent and educator, but the topic was on cuts, cuts, and more cuts to the budget.

When she shared her moment of insight with other educators, she exclaimed, "No wonder parents are not coming to meetings. They are tired, and their kids are hungry. They make the effort to attend, and then we bore them. We educators stick together and wonder why parents are not engaged with us. Shame on us." If we expect interaction with parents, we need to make that interaction valuable and important for them.

III

SUCCESS IS POSSIBLE

⑨

LEARNING FROM OTHERS' SUCCESS

WHAT RESEARCH SHOWS

Schools can use the best tools that research has to offer. Brain research, cooperative learning, and tools that come from business based on Arthur Deming's business model have been used by educators much to their delight. Successful schools adapt curricula to meet the students' specific needs. These schools realize that one size does not fit all but also that applying basic principles can help all students thrive and learn.

Some schools have already demonstrated that children who come from poverty can succeed. They have proven that poverty does not have to be a prescription for academic failure. They have shown that students who live in poverty can be strong scholars and successful students. They have found ways to lay powerful groundwork for children to develop the tools to be goal-oriented and fulfill their potential.

HIGH-PERFORMING, HIGH-POVERTY SCHOOLS

The Center for Public Education (2005) has identified that high-performing, high-poverty schools share certain traits. The faculty and staff of these successful schools believe that students can and will learn.

When you believe that a child can succeed, you talk to that child in a positive, affirming, and encouraging manner. Children respond to your image of them. You can create a vision for a child with the wonderful result that the child strives to live up to that vision. You create lessons that stretch the children's minds, and the children work to meet your expectations.

One lesson that successful parents learned is that as long as they were willing to do things for their children, their kids were more than willing to let their parent do it. If Mom always washed their clothes, why should they bother to learn how to take care of that task? If Dad always interceded for them when they had a disagreement with a friend or an adult, how would they ever learn to be responsible for their mistakes or misunderstandings? When parents inadvertently gave their children the message that they didn't think they could handle their own lives, the children proved the parents right.

When parents learn to expect their children to be responsible and learn basic survival skills, the children will develop those skills. The learning curve for parents and their children is not always smooth or easy, but with intentional effort, children have a chance to become responsible adults, spouses, and parents. Our expectations for children, low or high, lead them to live up to those measures. Our belief that they can be responsible individuals helps give them the potential to be responsible individuals.

High-performance, high-poverty schools use ongoing evaluations and assessments to ensure that students have the tools they need to succeed exactly when they need them. Lessons consistently change as needed to engage the students. In the early days of the adult education program at United Ministries (mentioned in chapter 7), the program had defined times for classes and attendance and homework requirements. The staff used prescribed curricula wherein students had to complete a variety of modules, no matter what the circumstances. The program outcomes for GEDs attained were disappointing, with approximately six to ten students earning their GEDs per year.

Students dropped out when they could not get to class and had too many absences. They got bored having to go over lessons that they already knew. They disengaged with the process the program staff had created. Finally, a bold and innovative program leader asked, "Why are we requiring people to spend time on lessons they have already mastered when, in reality, all they need is help in math or with writing or language skills? Why force them to waste their precious time?" This creative leader also asked why students had to come at particular times, times that created problems in terms of transportation and child care. The program's rules were forcing people to quit working on their GEDs.

After the adult education team wrestled with these questions, they realized that their rules and regulations impeded the students' success. They began testing students to identify weak areas and pointing students to materials and volunteer tutors who could help them improve in their areas of weakness. They allowed students to stop by when it was convenient for them. An additional benefit was that the staff no longer had to provide dinner, transportation, or child care to students because the adult students could now work around those issues. Today, the adult education program graduates more students than most high schools in the district.

High-performing, high-poverty schools use assessments to create curricula that meet or exceed the standards set for age appropriate learning. They do not "dumb down" the curricula, rather they develop ways to make the high expectations achievable. They expect their students to meet the high standards set for them and then work diligently to help them succeed.

High-performing, high-poverty schools use collaborative decision making among administrators, faculty, and staff. Just as teachers and students are partners in the learning experience, so are those responsible for these schools and what happens in them. Each brings unique insights, experiences, and knowledge, thereby making the final conception strong and viable. The flow of information and decision making is not top-down or bottom-up. It is always circular, with faculty, staff, and administrators working together to make sure their school and students remain stellar.

High-performing, high-poverty schools undergird the value of professional relationships among their faculty. Teachers work collaboratively across grade levels and subjects to ensure that students meet their goals and reach their full potential. Because they are all committed to their students, who they believe can and will learn, teachers and staff talk with each other to identify the specific needs of each child. They discover ways to unlock children's inquisitive minds through sharing their experiences and understandings of the child.

Just as a diamond has facets that make it sparkle in different ways depending on how light strikes it, children reveal different strengths and weaknesses to different teachers and staff members. Children will tell different pieces of their saga in different ways to different people. The cafeteria worker may have insights into a student that no teacher will ever know simply because the relationship is different. By working together, all the adults in a child's school life collaborate to develop a clearer picture of each student.

High-performing, high-poverty schools hire the best and most highly qualified teachers. Teachers are given the support they need to move beyond their usual ways of engaging students. The brightest, most experienced, and most creative teachers delight in unlocking the world of learning for their students. These teachers know that they are true catalysts in the lives of their students. Bright children who have many advantages may not truly appreciate the devotion and committed relationships with teachers that children who have so little need.

When I began my professional career as a teacher, I was given the students that no one else wanted to teach. I was young, looked even younger, and was inexperienced. My practice teaching in a small private school had not prepared me for the public school classroom that I walked into. I was overwhelmed with the challenges of my first teaching assignment. (Fortunately, teacher preparation has improved since then.) Looking back I have deep sympathy for my students. I didn't know what I was doing. They deserved better. They had been given a lesser education than they needed or deserved for success. They should have had the best teachers in the school rather than the greenest.

High-performing, high-poverty schools value interaction with the child's family. These schools find ways to engage parents, grandparents, aunts, uncles, and siblings and create the nurturing environment of enhanced and excited learning. (For more information, see chapter 8 on working with parents.)

TURNAROUND SCHOOLS

High-performing, high-poverty schools did not necessarily always have the same success they now enjoy. Some of them had to go through a turnaround process. A study funded by the Bill and Melinda Gates Foundation pinpointed some of the characteristics of turnaround schools (Calkins, Guenther, Belfiore, and Lash, 2007). The study found that to turn around their schools, administrative leaders had to recognize that they were facing tremendous challenges and that there was no "quick fix" through using the most current, state-of-the-art tool. They were not being asked to improve a school. They were being asked to turn around a school and adopt an entirely new way of functioning and educating students.

Some schools hired specialists to accomplish the task after realizing that people who had been functioning in the current system might not be able to step outside that system enough to see new ways, try different approaches, or push reluctant staff members to change. These turnaround specialists shared many of the skills that turnaround experts in business have.

Turnaround schools faced extensive fundamental change. The usual ways of thinking, planning, and implementing were no longer adequate and even counterproductive to the new vision. Turnaround schools can look very different from a traditional school because they do what works for their students. This is often radically different from the way they operated prior to the change.

Turnaround schools knew that their process required immediate modification. School leaders knew that whatever they did needed to happen right away. Ten years was far too long to wait to see results. Ten years is an entire generation of students. The sense of urgency was a powerful motivator that encouraged leaders to step out in bold, new ways. Turnaround schools wanted to see significant improvement within two years. The first year involved putting the processes into place and ensuring that everyone understood and was committed to the new vision for education. During year two, the processes and procedures were fully implemented and poor performance was not an option.

Leadership was shared in the turnaround schools. The principal was not the only change agent. Everyone was committed to creating an

optimal learning environment for students. There was a strong leadership team, but change belonged to every adult involved in the school,
including faculty, staff, volunteers, and even parents.

FLEXIBILITY AND CONTROL

Leaders in schools committed to the turnaround process had to be given
flexibility and control of many of the decisions regarding staff, budgeting, and programs. They could not be creative and bold if they were
forced to adhere to a system that had already been plagued by failure.
Although creativity was encouraged and expected, turnaround schools
were performance-based institutions. No one could just say "I'm doing a
good job." Each person was required to demonstrate that he was taking
the appropriate measures to demonstrate his strengths, as well as working on areas that needed improvement. Everyone put forth the effort to
bring about change because they were all committed to the turnaround
process.

Getting school districts to relinquish some of their power can be a
huge hurdle in some situations. An elementary school principal was
very frustrated because children who lived less than a mile from his
award-winning school were instead riding the bus to a school several
miles away. When he asked community leaders why children who lived
in the neighborhood were not attending the school built with them in
mind, he learned that many neighborhood parents needed to be at work
before school began each day. Although they liked what the new school
in their neighborhood was doing and they themselves wanted easy access to the school, they recognized that walking to school was not safe
for their children.

Because state law mandated that school buses could not transport
children if they lived within a one-mile radius of the school, the children
who lived in the immediate neighborhood had to walk to school. The
parents knew that for their children to attend the neighborhood school,
they had to leave home in the dark during the winter months. They had
to pass by many apartments, an especially scary thought for young children. The children also had to cross busy streets.

Parents needed to know that their children would arrive at school safely, and for them that meant having their children ride the bus. For most it was an easy decision when they opted for the school that provided bus service. Unfortunately for this principal, the rules remain unchanged, but his school still has a chance to be the change agent in the neighborhood that he wants it to be.

THIRD-PARTY PARTNERS

Some turnaround schools have learned that having a third-party partner committed to seeking change is helpful in achieving success. This partner might be a university, foundation, business, or nonprofit that commits to collaborating with the school and providing needed leadership for a period of two or three years or more. The partner invests in the turnaround process to ensure that it becomes a reality and that the process can sustain itself beyond the initial phases.

One example of a corporate partner is Michelin North America, a company with a 200-year commitment to bringing about change in our educational institutions. Dick Wilkerson, president and chief executive officer of Michelin North America, decided that the company would dedicate some of its resources to preparing schoolchildren for a lifetime of success. Wilkerson asked employees to volunteer their time to students to help them improve graduation rates and ready them to join the workforce. Each Michelin facility's employees have dedicated their time and efforts to a different school for partnerships.

When choosing schools to partner with, Michelin employees give priority to Title I and technological schools. Schools must have a culture where students are interested in moving forward and learning. The company requires a long-term commitment from school administrators and faculty. Founded in 2009, Michelin's Challenge Education has exceeded the expectations of both Michelin employees and school personnel.

East North Street Academy, identified in 1997 by the Greenville County School System as a magnet for mathematics and science to address issues of declining enrollment, achievement, and increasing minority isolation, partners with Michelin North America's corporate group.

In 1997, the magnet component began with 17 students. Today it is comprised of more than 150. The school itself has approximately 650 students, 61 percent of them being minority students.

More than 100 Michelin volunteers worked in the school during the first year of the partnership, a figure that ballooned to about 175 the following year. Volunteers worked as academic tutors providing one-on-one instruction. They assisted a math coach in preparing third, fourth, and fifth graders for math competitions and offered hands-on science activities in the science lab. They got involved in the after school program and served as breakfast and/or lunch buddies to students in need. They also sponsored a school store where "excellence bucks" could be used to purchase various items.[1]

When Bart Thompson, the engineer who designed the lunar wheel, met with students, he was able to add an element of "cool" to math and science. Thompson told the students, "When you make something new, you have to imagine all the ways it might be used. If you study math and science and understand how you can manipulate the laws of science, you can make things" (Munro, 2010, p. A1).

Schools can turn themselves around when there is the commitment to change, improvement, and success. For schools interested in embarking on this bold adventure, there are numerous studies and reports that describe the process and provide necessary information. Change is possible. Students who come from poverty do not have to be deprived of opportunity and success all their lives. Schools and school personnel can provide significant learning opportunities when there are parties with the boldness and willingness to confront the challenges.

COMMUNITY LEARNING CENTERS

The Riley Institute of Furman University conducted research funded by the William and Flora Hewlett Foundation to find out what people in South Carolina wanted for public education. What they learned pointed to the increasingly popular concept of public schools becoming community learning centers (Egelson, Culclasure, and James, 2010).

Community learning centers are often found in high-poverty, low-performing schools. These learning centers have several things in common and include "utilizing school facilities for multiple purposes to serve the community as a whole; serving students outside the traditional school day; integrating academic, health, arts, and recreational opportunities for students, parents, and community members; and offering academic and cultural enrichment to students at times when school is not in session" (Egelson, Culclasure, and James, 2010, p. 7).

One initiative was undertaken by Florence, South Carolina, County District Five. Johnsonville, South Carolina, is a small, rural community that lacks access to proper medical services. A nurse practitioner, Gaye Douglas, began caring for students in the school gym because there were no other options for health care in the community. Because she had also worked in an emergency room in a nearby town, she knew that people used hospital services for nonurgent medical needs because that was sometimes all that was available. Through a partnership with the school district, regional medical center, and Duke Endowment, the Campus Health Center was created. The center still works out of the gym but now serves the entire community.[2]

Other examples of excellent models for community learning centers are the Harlem Children's Zone Promise Academy in New York City, as well as a similar project in Denver, Colorado. While it is beyond the scope of this book to take an in-depth look at such programs, much has been written and is readily available about the Harlem's Children Zone. The Denver project began fourteen years ago when a local developer charged fees on all homes in his subdivisions to finance schools. One example of the Denver project is Green Valley Ranch. "Located on a 42-acre site, the school houses 750 K–8 students, has a 35,000-square-foot community recreation center, a community amphitheater, and a 21-acre regional park" (Egelson, Culclasure, and James, 2010, p. 12).

THE CAROLINA FIRST CENTER FOR EXCELLENCE

Attending workshops, studying research, and understanding how living in poverty can adversely affect a child's success in the classroom are foundational to successful teaching and learning. But sometimes you might be tempted to say, "All that's well and good, but what difference does this information make in my classroom? Sure, I can implement some of the changes that have been suggested in this material, but I'd really like some real-life examples."

One program that is proving its success is the Carolina First Center for Excellence educational program of the Greenville, South Carolina, Chamber of Commerce. Founded in 2001, the program now partners with 46 schools using Continuous Quality Improvement (CQI) tools. The program has equipped more than 18,000 schoolchildren with the analytical skills they need to serve as the building blocks for their academic future. The mission is to "change the way teachers teach and students learn by instituting CQI strategies in every classroom throughout Greenville County" (Greenville Chamber Foundation, 2009, p. 2).

The Carolina First Center for Excellence accomplishes its goal through a process that teaches students to set their own goals and solve problems. Teachers and students emphasize learning, not memorization. Because teachers and students use charts to demonstrate progress or identify areas that require more work, everyone who enters the school understands that this particular educational environment values goal setting and achievement.

For example, students use data notebooks to track their progress and establish goals beyond what they have already achieved. Each individual classroom also sets class goals so that everyone has a part in helping the class meet expectations. At the beginning of the year, each class sets a goal for the year. The mission for one class was, "We come to school so we can learn, so we can be smart, and learn to read, so we can go to college and be a doctor, vet, racecar driver, archeologist, or anything we want to be."

The Carolina First Center for Excellence has one overriding goal, and that is continued success. In the K–12 classrooms, students' vocabularies include flow charts, affinity diagrams, plus/delta, and consensograms. Students and teachers display data, tracking academic achievement and performance. Michele Brinn, director of the center, says "This method does not mandate a particular program, but places the focus on continuous improvements of district, school, and classroom processes. Students, teachers, and administrators enthusiastically embrace the CQI approach because they are not required to add one more thing to their plate, but they are provided tools and processes to evaluate what is on their plate, discard what is not working, and replace it with better and higher quality practices."

One of the special strengths of the Carolina First Center for Excellence approach is that it is not based on a win-lose process of acknowledging success by which children are ranked, making one the winner and the rest losers. With each child tracking his or her own progress, everyone is a winner, because everyone is working toward or beyond his or her personal best. When a room full of children is working on achieving a class goal, even the child who succeeds in getting two problems correct contributes to the overall class accomplishment.

Duncan Chapel Elementary as a Carolina First Center for Excellence Partner

Duncan Chapel Elementary is a Title I school in which 72% of the student body receive free and reduced lunches. Under the leadership of Regenia McClain, the school began using the Carolina First Center of Excellence approach in 2005. Upon entering the school, you realize right away that this is a school committed to quality. Just to the left of the front door in the lobby are the individual mission statements for each classroom. You immediately understand that the children who attend the school are committed to a mission, a mission that each of them had a part in developing and implementing.

The faculty, staff, and administrators commit the first two weeks of each school year to putting the code of conduct into place in the children's lives. Everyone quickly learns the great expectations and procedures of the school. Teachers review academic material during those two weeks as well, but they have learned that setting the foundation of high expectations, developing a common language, and helping all students learn acceptable behaviors sets the tone for everything that happens for the rest of the year.

When asked about how they handle disciplinary issues, instructional coach Nicki Thompson got a blank look on her face. She said that the two week focus on setting the academic, procedural, and behavioral expectations takes care of most problems, since they focus on goals, not conflict resolution. The younger children occasionally need more help in developing their internal controls for classroom behavior. Dawn Hawkins, also an instructional coach, gave the following example. She said that one first grade class described certain behaviors that inhibited learning by comparing the behaviors to those of animals. A child who talked a lot might be compared to buzzing like a bee. The follow-up question to a child might be, "What do you think you might do to help this bee buzz less?"

One little boy could not keep his hands to himself. It was pointed out to him that he was acting like an octopus. The teacher asked, "Do you think you could not act like an octopus? How long do you think you could practice not being an octopus? Fifteen minutes?" The child agreed that fifteen minutes sounded like a reasonable goal, so the teacher timed him. At the end of the fifteen minutes, he was complimented on his achievement. Then another fifteen-minute goal was set. The next time, the entire class cheered what he had been able to do.

Children track their own behavior each day on a color-coded sticker chart. They know where they stand based on the color sticker they earn. Green is positive, yellow means they have received a warning, red indicates that they need to stop what they are doing, and blue means that someone needs to be called in to help with the problem. As they chart their behavior, students must explain why they got a certain color and list things they can do to change it, if necessary. Every day starts anew.

Students focus on one behavioral goal at a time. When that goal is accomplished, the child chooses another goal. By doing so, they learn that they are part of a community in which everyone is working on personal goals as well as total class goals. All students track their reading and math goals.

Students maintain data notebooks that track behavior, academics, and sometimes even health goals. The notebooks belong to the children. When parents come to the school to meet with teachers, their child is in the conference as well. The child leads the conference, showing the parent the notebook and using it as a reference throughout the conference. Students describe their progress, areas in which they need improvement, and what they can do to meet their goals. When a child tells her mom that her reading might improve if Mom would read to her more, it's a powerful thing.

Teachers, administrators, and staff try to get to root causes of problems by using "The 5 Whys" strategy. Often by the time the fifth why is asked and answered, the teacher has developed some clarity regarding the problem. The following is an example of how a teacher might use the approach.

"Why are we in school?"	"To learn."
"Why do we need to learn?"	"So we can be smart."
"Why do we need to be smart?"	"So we can go to college."
"Why do we want to go to college?"	"So we can get a good job."
"Why do we want to have a good job?"	"So we can have a house, take care of our family, and be happy."

Then the teacher may refer the last answer back to the class mission statement so the student can develop an understanding of how everything that happens in the day connects with everything else.

Everyone at Duncan Chapel Elementary develops strategies based on agreed upon goals. Teachers, students, and parents alike come up with strategies. Students may have in-house mentors. A teacher may recognize that a child needs a special adult at school. Another teacher or staff person will volunteer to provide support to that child. By developing a relationship beyond the child's own classroom, that child feels enriched by the school's extensive personal and supportive relationships.

Duncan Chapel has also reached out to the community and pulled in multiple partners. They use school-based counselors from the Greenville Mental Health Center provided by Title I funding. After school programs are provided by a local nonprofit, Communities in Schools (21st Century Grant). This component offers peer mentor support, home visits, and parent nights. Through the Title I funds, the school has a parent involvement coordinator, a social worker, and an extra nurse.

During the summer, a state government-funded program, First Steps, provides two teachers who visit each incoming kindergarten student to assess student readiness. First Step teachers visit homes four times and bring the children and parents to the school on two occasions. A nonprofit provides book bags and supplies for the children and teachers show parents how to use the books and book bags with their children.

Duncan Chapel Elementary glows with the vision of its exemplary approach in helping each adult and child in the school succeed. Although they stand as a model in the school district, the administration and faculty are full of enthusiastic ideas of how they can continually improve their school and the lives of their students.[3]

GRADUATE GREENVILLE

When the Greenville, South Carolina, community realized that only 73.3% of its youth graduated high school within four years of entering the ninth grade, leaders knew that something had to be done. Through a partnership among United Way of Greenville County, the school district of Greenville County, and Public Education Partners of Greenville County, Graduate Greenville was created. The program targets eighth-grade students who demonstrate a spark for learning and success but who also have the potential to drop out of school or who may be at risk of failing a grade or course.

The rising ninth graders who are chosen for Graduate Greenville attend one of the five high schools that have Graduate Greenville graduation coaches. However, the crucial component of the program takes place the summer prior to entering ninth grade. During that summer, 20 to 25 students headed for each high school attend a four-week enrichment program at their new school.

According to Marge Scieszka, program director, the "morning curriculum includes 90 minutes of an algebra preparatory curriculum and 90 minutes of language arts, with an emphasis on literacy and writing skills. Teachers work with 10 to 12 students per class so that individual attention may be given. Afternoons involve a variety of activities, including working on study skills and character development, getting to know the high school, developing a sense of belonging at the school, and getting hands-on experiences in the arts. . . . On Fridays students do team-building exercises, visit local colleges and businesses . . . and engage in community service projects" (Graduate Greenville, 2010, n.p.).

When students enter school in the fall, they are already accustomed to their surroundings and have built a relationship with their graduation coach, who will work with them during the school year. The coach meets with each student weekly during the school year, gets to know the family through home visits, and connects with the student's teachers. The first-year program focus is for the student to earn enough credits to go to the tenth grade. Graduate Greenville staff operates with the belief that students who do not complete the ninth grade in one year are three times as likely to drop out.

At the end of the ninth grade, students who show great promise are invited to participate in Bridges to a Brighter Future, a program offered at Furman University. All Graduate Greenville students continue to work with their graduation coach until graduation. At the end of its fourth year, 74.5% of students enrolled in Graduate Greenville advanced to the next grade.

Since its inception, Graduate Greenville has also added a one-day community involvement component to its program. On the first Saturday after school begins, trained volunteers visit the homes of students who did not return to class at one of the five Graduate Greenville high schools. The volunteers give the students information on resources and other options that are available to them, for example, getting their GED. If students have barriers that prevent them from returning to school, the volunteers seek solutions. Students can go to their high school that Saturday to enroll and meet with graduation coaches and guidance counselors. One out of 10 students encouraged to return is in his or her desk the following Monday morning.

MULTIPLE LAYERS OF ATTACK

We must acknowledge that the issues associated with poverty require multiple layers of attack to achieve success. We can learn from the approaches of other communities if we truly want our quality of life to improve community wide. In chapter 5 you read about the children's medical clinic that has lawyers who contact patients' landlords to ask that they remove toxic substances and allergens from homes patients are living in. In that same clinic, hospital staff contact employers to inform them when an employee needs time off so that parents can bring their child in for a follow-up without the fear of losing their job (Shipler, 2005).These kinds of services are beyond the usual scope of medical clinics, but they are essential for the well-being of students who need the help to thrive.

A study done by Enterprise Community Partners in Maryland looked at the connection between healthy schools and community revitalization (Khadduri, Schwartz, and Turnham, 2008). The primary conviction uncovered by the study is that high-quality public education is an essential component of transforming distressed neighborhoods into healthy communities that can sustain themselves. Improving schools and empowering parents as the community rebuilds provides the tools for long-term positive growth.

The studies and factors considered in this chapter all point to the reality that solving the issues brought about by poverty requires a holistic, multilayered approach. We must provide quality education designed to meet these children's needs; housing that fosters safety, health, and opportunity; transportation that ensures independence and freedom of movement; and health care that is strong with medical providers who can move beyond the traditional approaches to medicine. We must also learn to acknowledge people's strengths rather than illuminate their weaknesses.

NOTES

1. Thanks to Steve Davis of Michelin North America for this valuable information.

2. For more information, contact Gaye Douglas at 843-386-2609, or at gdouglas@flo5.k12.sc.us or www.flo5.k12.sc.us.

3. A big thanks to Nikki Thompson and Dawn Hawkins at Duncan Chapel Elementary for their valuable insights.

(10)

CONCLUSION

Finding ways to connect with students who have different experiences and funds of knowledge can be both challenging and rewarding. To help solidify some of the lessons we've explored in this book, meet Abby, a single mom with two children. Abby grew up in a dysfunctional home where education was not valued. She felt lost both at home and at school, so she connected with people who introduced her to substances that relieved some of her sense of unworthiness and isolation. She dropped out of school at the age of sixteen because, as she said, no one at school reached out to her. She felt lost. She believed that it really didn't matter whether she stayed in school or not.

When Abby was in elementary school, she was fortunate in that she stayed at the same school through fifth grade. The teachers knew her and encouraged her because they saw that she was a bright student. One teacher noticed that Abby's shoes had loose soles and were flapping in the front and back. She pulled Abby out of line one day and said she'd take her to get some new shoes that afternoon. Abby was confused about what had just happened. Until that time, she had not noticed that her shoes were falling apart. She loved her new shoes with the alien puppet character Alf on them.

Abby remembers another painful time. All the children were asked to put their heads on the desk while a teacher checked their heads for lice. Those infested were asked to leave the classroom. No one could see who was tapped to leave because their heads were down, but they knew who was missing when they looked up after the checking process. With Abby's long, thick, curly hair, she was tapped regularly. Her mom could usually afford medication for one treatment but not for the follow-up. Without successive applications of the medicine, the lice could not be eliminated.

Abby says that school fund-raiser sales were also painful for her. She could not ask her neighbors to buy wrapping paper or candy because they were as poor as she was. When the fundraising was tied to how much an individual child had to pay for a field trip, she was doubly embarrassed. She couldn't sell enough to raise the money she needed, so the cost of special events became prohibitive for her.

When the washing machine broke in her home, the dirty clothes piled up. As a child, Abby did not know why no one sought other ways to wash clothes. She only knew that she had to wear the same clothes day after day. She still remembers the embarrassment she felt after one girl said, "You've worn that shirt four days in a row!" And that was Abby's favorite T-shirt.

A teacher planned a special field trip to a hibachi restaurant so the children could experience another culture. Abby was excited about this adventure, until she discovered that the cost was $16 per student. She knew to not to request that money at home. Every day the teacher would ask her about it, and Abby would say, "I forgot. I'll bring the money tomorrow." Finally, as the day drew near, Abby pretended that she did not care about the trip. She announced, "I'll just not go." The other students brought her back a "doggie bag" with noodles, but Abby still has not had that dining experience.

In middle school and high school, Abby changed schools frequently. In the ninth grade alone she went to three different schools. When she entered a new school, the textbook was usually the same, but the teacher used a different sequence. She was always either ahead or behind. She wishes now that the teachers would have made real efforts to reach out to new kids. Abby says that the kids who were in stable home environments received the attention they needed in class, but those who bounced from school to school were overlooked. Today she emphatically states that she knows it is hard to reach out when a teacher has 150 students, but she believes that being ignored is a key factor in why she dropped out. No one noticed.

Abby did not have lunch money, and her family did not apply for free lunches for her. She'd skip school to hang out at a fast food restaurant in hopes that she could talk another student into buying her food. Her grades plummeted. She learned to pretend that she didn't care about anything to reduce her overwhelming embarrassment.

Abby was later arrested on a felony drug charge. While she was in jail, she missed her daughter's third birthday and also discovered that she was pregnant with her son. Having time to sit and think, she realized that she'd just received a huge wake-up call to live her life in new and different ways. The judge told her that if she did community service hours, her record would be expunged, and because this judge was enlightened, he allowed Abby to work off her hours by attending an adult education program.

It was while earning her GED that Abby finally found a role model who saw the amazing potential in her. Janey told Abby that she could accomplish anything she decided to do. Even when Abby got discouraged, Janey believed in her and inspired her along the journey. Janey talked with Abby about her choices, relationships, work, and studies. She was the supportive role model that Abby had yearned for all her life. When Abby was awarded her GED, Janey was right there, encouraging her to continue her education.

Abby enrolled in the local technical college and returned to get help from Janey when a subject was overwhelming. She received a work study scholarship that allowed her to help other students earn their GEDs. As she became stronger in her abilities, she left the abusive relationship that she had depended on for so long. She continued to work and nurture her children while working on first her associate's degree and then her bachelor's.

Abby's daughter excels in school because her mom encourages her along the way. Even when her daughter needs a time-out, Abby uses that time productively. Her second grade daughter works on her multiplication tables while sitting in her time-out chair. At the time of this writing, Abby's daughter had scored higher in math than any other child at her school.

Abby appreciates the fact that the teacher asked Abby, not her daughter, if she might need supplies for a science fair. Abby quips, "It takes money to be creative. I'm glad that the teacher did not place my daughter in an uncomfortable position and asked me instead if we needed chenille sticks and a shoe box for a diorama." Her son will also benefit from having such an involved and passionate mother when he enters school.

Abby has turned her life around in amazing ways. She now accepts her past, while embracing her future. She shares her story to inspire others to make better choices for themselves and their families. We can celebrate her successes.

One question lingers: How would Abby's life be different if she had received early and consistent support to overcome the obstacles in her life? Fortunately, Abby found the support and education she craved before she created obstacles that might have been impossible to overcome. Who are the Abbys in your classroom? Will you open your heart and mind to understanding how poverty affects them and reach out to help these children succeed in life?

Appendix A

SETTING UP A POVERTY TOUR

A great way to encourage people to bring change to your community is to take them on a poverty tour and show them the "other side" of your community. Such a tour can demonstrate how close poor neighborhoods are to the same neighborhoods that they frequent on a daily basis. It can also help open their eyes to parts of your city or county that many residents may not even know exist.

Developing a poverty tour takes some time and research, but helping others see with their eyes, smell with their noses, and feel in their gut is worth the time investment. Once people know that you will take them out to learn, you will have many opportunities to share this important experience.

The first step in developing a poverty tour is to identify the neighborhoods and areas that you want to include. Look for neighborhoods that are known to have high concentrations of people living in poverty. You can identify them in several ways, including the following:

- Ask people who run or participate in programs for those with limited resources.
- Look at tax records for properties with a low tax base and the ratio of home ownership to rental.

- Ask city officials which neighborhoods are targeted for redevelopment.
- Ask public and/or affordable housing professionals.
- Ask teachers, social workers, health care professionals who do home visits.
- Ask people who work with the homeless.
- Get in your car and drive around. If you move two or three blocks off of the main thoroughfares, you will usually find streets that are home to high concentrations of people living in poverty. Explore your own community with new eyes.

The second step is to learn about the history of the neighborhoods that you want to include on your tour. Were they developed to be low-income communities? If not, what happened? Who abandoned the neighborhood? You can often get this information from local history buffs, including professors, historic preservationists, genealogists, and so forth. If you're lucky, your local or state university library will have books or documents that detail the history of the area. Long-time residents are also often willing to share their experiences.

You may also want to consider the policies, ordinances, and laws that undergird the existence of neighborhoods that can only be described as blighted. You might offer the premise that laws are made by people to protect the people who make the laws. For example, the old Jim Crow laws in the South that separated white people from black people were made by white people. Those laws certainly did not benefit black people, but significant numbers of white people felt safer and more comfortable having those laws in place. Discuss how laws benefit those who make them and hurt, either intentionally or inadvertently, those who do not have such power.

Find out what the units in the neighborhoods you are touring usually rent for by contacting the landlords who have posted For Rent signs on the buildings or by calling housing counselors in your area. The issue of "slum lords" might warrant some research. As you drive people around the neighborhoods, tour participants may begin blaming the owners of the rental properties for the bad conditions of the houses. Some landlords certainly ignore the state of their housing but still charge a high fee for rent. They add to the victimization of residents in the community by demanding large sums of money and providing minimal services. If you look at tax rolls to discover who owns the properties, you may be horrified at some of the names you see.

Conversely, some owners really do want to maintain their property. They may put kitchen appliances in the unit only to have them stolen. After replacing the appliances two or three times, they might quit trying to provide a refrigerator or stove. At other times, replacing a furnace might necessitate raising the rent to cover the costs of repairs, in addition to the taxes and insurance the landlord pays. The landlord might choose to provide housing to the current tenant at an affordable rate rather than force the tenant to move due to insufficient funds. The landlord might also prefer to tear down existing units to build new ones to code, but building to code may require that two units on contiguous lots be torn down to accommodate the one replacement unit, thus removing one more housing option. Sometimes the cost of repairs necessitates that the unit be priced out of the range for the neighborhood.

The issue of low-income rental property has a lot of gray areas. As one landlord who is committed to justice said, "Someone has to provide this housing. I choose to do it, but I must also make some money to be able to do it. I am not a charity." Another landlord quipped, "Bad housing is better than no housing or better than living in a car." This last comment is certainly open to discussion. Simply blaming the landlords does not get to the deeper understandings of how this kind of housing happened in the first place and what regulations hinder major improvements.

The third step is to identify which points you will highlight on the tour. If you discover paths into wooded areas or bamboo thickets, look carefully for evidence of human habitation, for example, clothing or sleeping bags, makeshift roofs made of cardboard or tarpaulins, cans and bottles, and so forth. Homeless people might also live under shrubs and bridges.

If you see satellite dishes attached to apartment buildings or houses that are obviously home to people who are poor, help the tour participants understand that these people may have satellite dishes on their apartments for numerous reasons. Entertainment is typically very important to people who have low incomes, and immigrants, especially those who come from Spanish-speaking countries, like to keep up with news from home and watch programs in their own language.

Look at the churches in the communities. Are there many of them? What denominations are there? Does the number of churches undergird or dispel the notion that people who are poor are not religious?

If you find houses that are dilapidated but that have a nice car parked in the driveway, offer the understanding that it is much easier to get a car loan than a house loan. Most people might not know where someone lives, but they will notice the car someone drives to work, to visit relatives and friends, to attend church, and so on.

If some houses have tiny rooms attached to the rear, they are likely bathrooms that were required additions when outdoor plumbing was discontinued by government ordinance. In some communities, the ordinance required that city water be run to the house, not into the house, just to the house. The people living in the house might not have had the resources to connect the water, or the landlord might not have chosen to attach the water. Many of the add-on bathrooms have only a toilet and a sink, and they may or may not be connected to the water and/or sewer system. A number of these connected bathrooms originally had a door that opened only to the outside of the house.

If you see wooden pallets piled in a yard, assume that this is firewood. Some locales do not require landlords to furnish heat. The ordinance might require that if the unit has a heat source, it must be functional. No heat means that the resident is required to heat with wood in a fireplace (wooden pallets, which are used for firewood, are made from pine, which is high in creosote and liable to cause chimney fires) or with kerosene (which leaves clothing with a distinctive odor).

Houses with boarded up windows and doors may have people living in them, even if they do not have electricity or water. Notice whether the boards covering doorways are actually nailed up or if they are simply leaning on the door. Boards may be loose at windows to allow access inside. Occasionally the windows will be boarded up and the door will be standing wide open. Abandoned buildings often provide shelter for people who have nowhere else to go.

Pay attention to what is different about low-wealth neighborhoods. In addition to the houses being small, old, and in a state of disrepair, they may lack sidewalks, gutters, lighting, and driveways. Trash may be piled on the side of the street. Roads may be extremely narrow. Do people on the tour notice these things? Ask what is missing from the neighborhood and let them see for themselves the discrepancies between where they live and where people who are poor and who have limited options are living. Does this neighborhood feel safe for children? Why or why not? What are the implications for the futures of children raised in these conditions?

The fourth step is to engage your tour participants so they can be inspired to do something with what they have seen. Remind them that the current residents in the neighborhoods you are touring did not cause the present conditions. Circumstances, often beyond their control, resulted in the blight that is now obvious. People with decision-making power in the past helped create these neighborhoods, for good or ill. Lack of government services, such as infrequent garbage pick-up, lead to more and more garbage being dumped. The lack of voice of the residents limits vision and appropriate improvements.

Encourage tour participants to write letters to their state officials, get involved with community groups who are trying to make a difference, encourage other people to go on the tour, suggest that their faith community develop a presence in the community, and so forth. If someone suggests that the tour has the feel of going through a zoo and that he or she is embarrassed, listen empathetically and affirm their feelings. Then offer the alternative understanding that until people see what is in their own community, they will feel no compulsion to do anything about it. Hiding behind our embarrassment does not help us become motivated to change the conditions our neighbors are being forced to live in.

Go to the National Low-Income Housing Coalition's website at www .nlich.org for more information specific to your county. Their "Out of Reach" section provides vital facts about any area in the country.

One final step is to always pay attention to safety issues. Know where it is safe to stop your tour vehicle and those areas that you should avoid. Taking private cars is not as safe as taking a vehicle that is clearly marked as belonging to an agency, school, or congregation. Know where it is safe to get out and walk around and where you should stay inside the vehicle. Keep the doors locked at all times.

While these precautions are important, if you become known in a community as someone who cares and who is trying to make a difference, people might actually wave to you as you drive by. But we must always remember that these neighborhoods, because of their neglect, attract people who have mental health issues, who are addicts, and who are involved in criminal activity. These are the same folks whom the longtime residents would like have removed from their communities. They do not want to live close to these dangers any more than you or I do.

Appendix B

PROGRESS REPORT

When a child gets an F on a paper, that's that. There is no way for the child to undo the grade if the instructional system is set up so that the child only has one attempt to learn something. This F can act as negative feedback that halts all feelings of motivation. When a grading system is based on a 10-point scale, with 90–100 being an A, 80–89 being a B, and so on, the range for an F is huge (0–59). It can seem impossible for the child to overcome his or her failure, and this feeling can serve to reinforce any negative and failure-oriented thoughts that the child already has.

Another format that works for some schools (including Carolina First Center for Excellence partner schools) is to have daily and/or weekly progress charts that are maintained by students. For example, suppose a math worksheet has ten problems. The teacher's goal is for the students to get eight problems right. Imagine a graph on which the vertical line represents the number of problems (0–10), and the horizontal line illustrates the days of the week (Monday through Friday). A dotted horizontal line begins at the number eight and runs across all the days of the week.

Suppose that on Monday, the student gets 1 problem correct. She colors in a bar that extends to the number 1. On Tuesday's worksheet, she gets to the number 2. It is easy for her to see that she is making progress. This is much more positive and means much more to her than focusing on the fact that she missed eight problems. Say on Wednesday she gets five correct, but on Thursday slips back to three. Now she sees that she has lost some ground. The teacher can then ask the student what her plans are for getting the line on her graph to go back up. Because the teacher has already worked with all students to plan strategy, the student might say, "I'll have to work harder." Teachers report that students rarely have a line that drops down on the graph two times in a row.

REFERENCES

Adelman, L. (2008). *Unnatural Causes: Is Inequality Making Us Sick?* 240 min. San Francisco, CA: California Newsreel, with Vital Pictures.

Allen, V. "What Can You Buy with Food Stamps?" Dec. 10, 2008, http://www.helium.com/items/1262622-what-can-you-buy-with-food-stamps

American Fact Finder, U.S. Census Bureau http://factfinder.census.gov/servlet/STTable?_bm=y&-geo_id=01000US&-qr_name=ACS_2009_5YR_G00_S0101&-ds_name=ACS_2009_5YR_G00_

Ascher, C., and Fruchter, N. (2001, July). Teacher Quality and Student Performance in New York City's Low-Performing Schools. *Journal of Education for Students Placed at Risk,* 6(3), 199–214.

Barth, P., Haycock, K., Jackson, H., Mora, K., Ruiz, P., Robinson, S., and Wilkins, A. (1999). *Dispelling the Myth: High-Poverty Schools Exceeding Expectations.* Washington, DC: Education Trust.

Bartle, P. (2010, March 24). Factors of Poverty: The Big Five. Retrieved September 17, 2010, from www.scn.org/cmp/modules/emp-pov.htm.

Berne, E. (2010). Transactional Analysis: Early TA History and Theory. Retrieved October 19, 2010, from www.businessballs.com/transact.htm.

Calkins, A., Guenther, W., Belfiore, G., and Lash, D. (2007). The Turnaround Challenge: Why America's Best Opportunity to Dramatically Improve Student Achievement Lies in Our Worst-Performing Schools. Retrieved September 17, 2010, from www.massinsight.org/stg/research/challenge/.

Carollo, C., and McDonald, H. (2002). *What Works with Low-Performing Schools: A Review of Research*. Charleston, WV: AEL.

Carter, S. C. (2000). *No Excuses: Lessons from 21 High-Performing, High-Poverty Schools*. Washington, DC: Heritage Foundation.

Center for Public Education. (2005, August). Key Lessons: High-Performing, High-Poverty Schools. Retrieved September 3, 2010, from www.centerfor publiceducation.org/site/c.goJQI0OwElH/b.2119183/k.90B9/key_lessons _highperforming_highpoverty_schools.htm.

Chenoweth, D. (2007, May). The Economic Cost of Substandard Housing Conditions among North Carolina Children. Retrieved October 19, 2010, from www.nlihc.org/doc/repository/NC-HC-report4-30-08.pdf.

Child Trends. (2010). Child Trends Databank. Retrieved September 17, 2010, from www.childtrendsdatabank.org.

Delaney, E. M., and Kaiser, A. P. (1996). The Effects of Poverty on Parenting Young Children. *Peabody Journal of Education*, 71(4), 66–85. Retrieved September 17, 2010, from www.jstor.org/pss/1493185.

Eckholm, E. (2008, June 24). To Avoid Student Turnover, Parents Get Rent Help. *New York Times*. Retrieved September 17, 2010, from www.nytimes .com/2008/06/24/us/24move.html.

Egelson, P., Culclasure, B., and James, A. (2010). Transforming Schools into Community Learning Centers. Retrieved October 19, 2010, from http://riley .furman.edu/education/transforming-schools-community-learning-centers.

Every Child Matters Education Fund (2008, April). Geography Matters: Child Well-Being in the States. Retrieved September 17, 2010, from www.every childmatters.org/storage/documents/pdf/reports/geomatters.pdf.

Florida Department of Education (2009, September). Free/Reduced-Price Lunch Eligibility. Retrieved May 13, 2010, from www.fldoe.org/eias/eiaspubs/ pdf/frplunch.pdf.

Gans, H. J. (1971, July/August). The Uses of Poverty: The Poor Pay All. Retrieved February 21, 2009, from www.sociology.org.uk/as4p3.pdf.

Graduate Greenville. (2010). What We Do. Retrieved October 19, 2010, from www.graduategreenville.org/index.php.

Gray, J. (1992). *Men Are from Mars, Women Are from Venus*. New York: Harper Collins.

Greenville Chamber Foundation (2009). *Carolina First Center for Excellence*. Greenville, SC: Chamber of Commerce.

Haley, A. (1965). *The Autobiography of Malcolm X*. New York: Ballantine Books.

Kagan, S., and Kagan, M. (1994). *Cooperative Learning*, 2nd ed. San Clemente, CA: Kagan Publishing.

Kannapel, P. J., Clements, S. K., Kannapel, D., and Hibschman, T. (2005, February). Inside the Black Box of High-Performing Schools. Retrieved December 4, 2007, from www.cdl.org/resource-library/pdf/FordReportJE .pdf.

Karelis, C. (2007). *The Persistence of Poverty: Why the Economics of the Well-Off Can't Help the Poor.* New Haven, CT: Yale University Press.

Khadduri, J., Schwartz, H., and Turnham, J. (2008). A Policy Roadmap for Expanding School-Centered Community Revitalization. Retrieved September 17, 2010, from www.practitionerresources.org/cache/documents/669/66901 .pdf.

Linehan, M. F. (1992, September). Children Who Are Homeless: Educational Strategies for School Personnel. Retrieved September 17, 2010, from www .eric.ed.gov/ERICWebPortal/search/detailmini.jsp?_nfpb=true&_&ERICE xtSearch_SearchValue_0=EJ449878&ERICExtSearch_SearchType_0= no&accno=EJ449878 (EJ449878).

Liz Library. (2009). Parenting and Children's Educational Achievement: Myths and Facts about Parental Involvement. Retrieved September 17, 2010, from www.thelizlibrary.org/liz/021.htm.

McCormick, L., and Holden, R. (1992, September). Homeless Children: A Special Challenge. *Young Children,* 47(6), 61–67. Retrieved September 17, 2010, from www.eric.ed.gov/ERICWebPortal/search/detailmini.jsp?_nfpb= true&_&ERICExtSearch_SearchValue_0=EJ451993&ERICExtSearch _SearchType_0=no&accno=EJ451993 (EJ451993).

Missouri Association for Community Action (2010). Community Action Poverty Simulation. Jefferson: Missouri Association for Community Action.

Moll, L. C., Amanti, C., Neff, D., and Gonzalez, N. (2001). Funds of Knowledge for Teaching: Using a Qualitative Approach to Connect Homes and Classrooms. *Theory into Practice,* 2(31), 133.

Munro, J. (2010, February 20). Awesome. *The Greenville News,* p. A1.

National Center for Children in Poverty (2010). Parents' Low Education Leads to Low Income, Despite Full-Time Employment. Retrieved February 14, 2007, from www.nccp.org.

National Center for Children in Poverty (2010). Wigth, V., Chau, M., and Aratani, Y. "Who are America's Poor Children?" http://nccp.org/publications/pub-912.html

National Consumer Law Center (2008) Wu, C., and Fox, J. "Coming Down: Fewer Refund Anticipation Loans, Lower Prices from Some Providers, But Quickie Tax Refund Loans Still Burden the Working Poor," http://www .consumerfed.org/elements/www.consumerfed.org/file/finance/RAL_2008 _Report_final.pdf

National Low Income Housing Coalition (2009). Out of Reach 2009. Retrieved September 17, 2010, from www.nlihc.org/oor/oor2009/.

National Poverty Center of University of Michigan (2009), http://npc.umich.edu/poverty

Payne, R. K. (2005). *A Framework for Understanding Poverty*. Highlands, TX: Aha! Process.

Pellino, K. M. (2007). Effects of Poverty on Teaching and Learning. Retrieved September 17, 2010, from www.teach-nology.com/tutorials/teaching/poverty/print.htm.

Ragland, M. A., Clubine, B., Constable, D., and Smith, P. A. (2002, April). Expecting Success: A Study of Five High-Performing, High-Poverty Schools. Retrieved September 17, 2010, from www.eric.ed.gov/ERICWeb Portal/search/detailmini.jsp?_nfpb=true&_&ERICExtSearch_SearchValue_ 0=ED468010&ERICExtSearch_SearchType_0=no&accno=ED468010 (ED468010).

Rexrode, C. "Mortgage Interest Tax Break a Sacred Cow?" March 16, 2011, http://www.pittsburghtrib/business/s_725999.html

Shipler, D. (2005). *The Working Poor: Invisible in America*. New York: Vintage Books.

Slavin, R. E. (1997–1998, December/January). Can Education Reduce Social Inequity? *Educational Leadership*, 4(55), 6–10. Retrieved July 16, 2001, from www.ascd.org/publications/educational-leadership/dec97/vol55/num04/Can-Education-Reduce-Social-Inequity.aspx.

Slocumb, P. D., and Payne, R. (2000, May). Identifying the Gifted Poor. *New Diversity*, 5(79), 28–32. Retrieved July 10, 2001, from www.nagc.org/index .aspx?id=656.

U.S. Department of Agriculture, Economic Research Service (2008). Nord, M., Andrews, M., and Carlson, S. (2009) "Household Food Security in the United States, 2008." http://www.ers.usda.gov/publications/err83/

Templeton, B. L. (2008). *Loving Our Neighbor: A Thoughtful Approach to Helping People in Poverty*. Bloomington, NY: iUniverse.

Thackray, J. (2010). The Gallup Q12. Retrieved September 3, 2010, from www .artsusa.org/pdf/events/2005/conv/gallup_q12.pdf.

Tough, P. (2006, November). What It Takes to Make a Student. Retrieved September 17, 2010, from www.nytimes.com/2006/11/26/magazine/26tough .html?pagewanted=print.

University of Victoria. (1995, September). Levels of Usage: The UVIC Writer's Guide. Retrieved April 6, 2010, from http://web.uvic.ca/wguide/Pages/SentLevsUsage.html.

U.S. Department of Health and Human Services (2010). http://aspe.hhs.gov/poverty/09poverty.shtml

Vandivere, S., Hair, E. C., Theokas, C., Cleveland, K., McNamara, M., and Atienza, A. (2006). How Housing Affects Child Well-Being. Retrieved September 18, 2010, from www.fundersnetwork.org/usr_doc/Housing_and _Child_Well_Being.pdf.

Virtual Museum of Canada. (2002). Storytelling: Oral Tradition. Retrieved April 12, 2010, from www.virtualmuseum.ca/Exhibitions/Holman/english/storytelling/index.php3.

Whitfield, R., Parker, G., and Childress, T. W. (1992). *Adult Basic Skills Instructor Training Manual*. Boone, NC: Appalachian State University.

ABOUT THE AUTHOR

Beth Lindsay Templeton, director of Our Eyes Were Opened, is a community activist, innovator, minister and presbytery leader, consultant, teacher, and writer. She began her career as a secondary mathematics teacher. For more than 28 years, she has worked at United Ministries, a nonprofit in Greenville, South Carolina. She has interacted with people who are poor and marginalized, as well as with groups and individuals who want to help people with minimal resources. She is the author of *Loving Our Neighbor: A Thoughtful Approach to Helping People in Poverty* and the poverty expert in an EcuFilm DVD series titled *Servant or Sucker*. She is a graduate of Presbyterian College and Erskine Theological Seminary. She and her husband have three married sons and four grandchildren.